It's Another Ace Book from CGP

This book is for everyone taking <u>GCSE English</u>.

It uses plain simple language to explain all the tricky stuff about English grammar, so it's really easy to read and revise from.

It's not all dreary facts either. We've added a good sprinkling of silly bits to keep you awake and maybe even mildly amused.

CGP are just the best

The central aim of Coordination Group Publications is to produce top quality books that are carefully written, immaculately presented and marvellously funny — whilst always making sure they exactly cover the National Curriculum for each subject.

And then we supply them to as many people as we possibly can, as cheaply as we possibly can.

Buy our books — they're ace

Contents

SECTION FOUR — WHAT A SENTENCE IS

SECTION FIVE — WRITING BETTER SENTENCES

SECTION SIX — PARAGRAPHS

SECTION SEVEN — COMMONLY CONFUSED WORDS

SECTION EIGHT — LAZY MISTAKES

Published by Coordination Group Publications
Typesetting, layout and illustrations by The English Coordination Group

Contributors:
Written and Co-edited by Simon Cook BA (Hons)
Design, graphics and additional writing by James Wallis BEng (Hons)
Additional illustrations by Lex Ward

ISBN   1-84146-111-3

Groovy website: www.cgpbooks.co.uk

Jolly bits of clipart from CorelDRAW.

Printed by Elanders Hindson, Newcastle upon Tyne.

1200

The Four Kinds of Noun

This is where it all starts. A noun is a word that tells you the name of a person or thing. 'Paul', 'cat', 'Scotland' and 'turnip' are all nouns.

Remember the Four Kinds of Noun

1) These ones are proper names. They all have capital letters.

See P.29 for more on these ones.

John, Spain, the Arts Council, Tuesday, July, Cardiff

2) Then there are common names of things or places — just everyday words really.

plant, woman, house, forest, horse, bus

3) Some special words are names for groups of people or things.

Penguin flock largin' it tonight, man.

Big up to the penguin massive.

class, team, club, herd, flock, squad

4) Here are the tricky ones. These are words for ideas — things you can't see, hear or touch.

rage, truth, beauty, sadness, love, fear

You Only Need to Know About Using Nouns

If that lot sounds a bit technical, don't worry. It's the easiest way to show you what a noun is. The thing you need to learn is how to use nouns properly — especially when there's more than one person or thing involved.

The ship chased the whale.

The ships chased the whales.

A rose by any other name — a flower perhaps...

This stuff is basic information to help make the first section clearer. You don't need to know any complicated facts about nouns — they're naming words for ideas, groups, people and things.

Forming the Plural of Nouns

When you have <u>two or more</u> of something, you need to <u>change</u> the noun to a <u>plural</u> form. That's where lots of people <u>mess up</u>. Make sure you <u>learn</u> the right plural <u>spellings</u> now.

Most *Words Add '-s' to Make the* Plural

This is easy: <u>rat</u> + <u>-s</u> = more than one rat.

The rat<u>s</u> leapt into the sea.

And again: <u>sailor</u> + <u>-s</u> = more than one sailor.

The sailor<u>s</u> jumped too.

There are *Two Plural Forms* for Words that *End in '-y'*

1) Look at the letter in <u>front</u> of the '<u>-y</u>'.
   If it's a <u>vowel</u> — a, e, i, o, u — just <u>add '-s'</u>.

key ➡ key<u>s</u>   tray ➡ tray<u>s</u>

2) If the letter in <u>front</u> of the '<u>-y</u>' is a <u>consonant</u>: <u>chop off</u> the '-y' and stick on '<u>-ies</u>'.

party ➡ part<u>ies</u>   fly ➡ fl<u>ies</u>

Be careful with <u>people's names</u> that end in '<u>-y</u>' — you just <u>add</u> an '<u>-s</u>' for the plural.

I went to see the Brady<u>s</u>.   The Kennedy<u>s</u> were famous.

Some Words *Stay the Same in the* Plural

sheep ➡ <u>sheep</u>   fish ➡ <u>fish</u>

I can only manage one at a time, myself.

<u>Don't</u> write 'fishes' — it's <u>really old-fashioned</u>.

Tricky Plural Spellings

Some plurals can get really tricky. There's nothing for it but to learn them, I'm afraid.

Some Words Need '-es' or You Can't Say Them

1) You can't just add '-s' to these words — they're impossible to say.

NO!

box + '-s' = boxs   glass + '-s' = glasss   watch + '-s' = watchs

2) You've got to add '-es' for the correct plural.

box**es**   glass**es**   watch**es**

You've got to add '-es' for the plurals of any words ending in '-s', '-z', '-sh', '-tch' and '-x'.

Most Words Ending in '-o' Add '-s'

piano → piano**s**
disco → disco**s**

You'll have to learn these exceptions too — they always add '-es'.

potato**es**   tomato**es**   echo**es**   hero**es**

Most Words Ending in '-f' and '-fe' Change to '-ves'

life ➡ li**ves**   leaf ➡ lea**ves**   shelf ➡ shel**ves**

It's my favourite hoof of all my hooves.

But you must learn these awkward ones that keep the '-f'.

chie**fs**   belie**fs**   proo**fs**   roo**fs**

Other Words Have Completely Different Plurals

wom**a**n ➡ wom**e**n   m**ou**se ➡ m**i**ce   oas**is** ➡ oas**es**

More than one questionnaire — plural forms...

Phew — loads of stuff to learn here. The secret is to take it slowly. Look at each rule in turn and scribble it down in rough. Make sure you understand it totally before you move on to the next one.

Pronouns

This is where all that business about <u>nouns</u> comes in <u>handy</u>.
<u>Pronouns</u> are words you use <u>instead</u> of nouns, so you <u>don't</u> keep <u>repeating</u> the same dull words.

Pronouns *Take the* Place *of* Nouns

There's something <u>weird</u> about this sentence. You really <u>don't</u> need to <u>repeat</u> the name '<u>Max</u>'.

> *Max had ten seconds to save the world,*
> *but as <u>Max</u> reached for the key, the screen went blank...*

This sounds more <u>natural</u>. Instead of writing Max again, use a <u>pronoun</u> — '<u>he</u>'.

> *Max had ten seconds to save the world,*
> *but as <u>he</u> reached for the key, the screen went blank...*

It's all <u>obvious</u> stuff here — you do it all the time.
This is just to <u>make sure</u> you've got it <u>clear</u> in your mind.

Pronouns *Change Form* too — *Learn* These Ones *First*

1) Here are some of the simple pronouns you use <u>all the time</u> — I, you, he/she/it, we, they.

> *<u>I</u> know that <u>you</u> love skiing.*

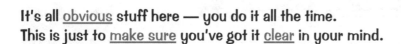

2) You need these forms because '<u>I</u>' and '<u>you</u>' are <u>doing</u> the actions in this sentence.

> *<u>They</u> think it's odd that <u>we</u> go uphill.*

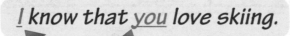

3) Same in this example — '<u>they</u>' and '<u>we</u>' are <u>doing</u> something.

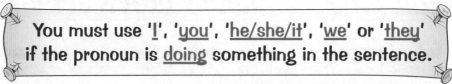

> You must use '<u>I</u>', '<u>you</u>', '<u>he/she/it</u>', '<u>we</u>' or '<u>they</u>'
> if the pronoun is <u>doing</u> something in the sentence.

Just pro-nouns — no amateurs allowed...

This may all <u>seem</u> really <u>easy</u>, but that's why you need to <u>go over it</u>. One of the <u>big secrets</u> of doing well in your GCSE is <u>cutting out</u> any <u>silly mistakes</u>. Check this lot over and get it all <u>learned</u>.

More Pronouns

That isn't the end of the story. These pronouns change when you use them for different things. This is where you can make some serious mistakes — keep your eyes open and learn this page.

Learn When to Use These Common Forms Instead

1) This is a pronoun too — it's like 'I' but it'd be wrong to say "Don't bump into I again."

   Don't bump into me again.

2) Here's a tougher one. 'He' is a pronoun but so is 'her'.

   He went straight into her.

3) You've got to use 'he' because he is doing the action.
   She isn't doing anything, so you've got to use 'her' instead.

   The notes aren't yours, they look like mine.

4) Three pronouns here. 'They' are doing the action.
   'Mine' means something belongs to me, and 'yours' means something belongs to you.

Don't Get these Different Pronouns Muddled

You need these pronouns when there's one person:

These ones are for when the person has something done to them.

These are for when the person is doing something.

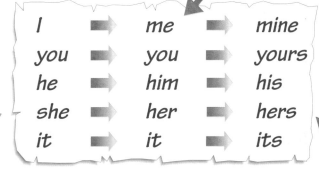

I	➡	me	➡	mine
you	➡	you	➡	yours
he	➡	him	➡	his
she	➡	her	➡	hers
it	➡	it	➡	its

These ones are for when something belongs to the person.

You've got to use these ones when there's more than one person:

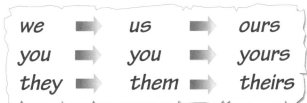

we	➡	us	➡	ours
you	➡	you	➡	yours
they	➡	them	➡	theirs

A place for coal digging — it's all mine...

You've really got to get these two pages learned. Don't forget you use the pronoun 'it' for things.

6

Mistakes with 'I' and 'Me'

These two pronouns can be a big hassle if you aren't careful.
The only way to avoid any silly mistakes is by learning this page thoroughly.

Don't Use 'Me' When You Mean 'I'

1) This sentence is wrong.

> *Ned and me chased the taxman.*

"70%? You swine!"

2) Break it up into two sentences and you'll see why.

> *Ned chased the taxman.*   = fine

> *Me chased the taxman.*   = WRONG

3) You can't say 'me chased' but you can say 'I chased the taxman.'

> *Ned and I chased the taxman.*

4) Much better. This time the sentence is right.

> If the pronoun is doing something, you can't use 'me', you need 'I' instead.

5) And remember — the 'I' or 'me' always comes second.

> *They came to see me and Pat.*   NO!

> *They came to see Pat and me.*

6) When there's someone else, their name always goes first.

After 'Between' or 'With' You Must Use 'Me'

These two sentences sound very grand but they're completely wrong.   NO!

> *Between you and I, this is wrong.*

> *She came to the party with Dan and I.*

When you use words like 'between', 'with' or 'to', you've got to use 'me'.

> *Between you and me, this is wrong.*

> *She came to the party with Dan and me.*

Between you and me — him, her, it, us & them...

Learn this — use 'I' if the pronoun is doing something, but use 'me' after 'between', 'with' and 'to'.

Using 'Who' and 'Which'

These are two words that you'll <u>definitely</u> need for your written work.
All you need to do is learn <u>when</u> to use them properly, so that you <u>don't</u> muddle them up.

There are <u>Two Main Ways</u> You Use 'Who' and 'Which'

1) You need '<u>who</u>' and '<u>which</u>' for questions.

<u>Who</u> was that?　　<u>Which</u> is your favourite?

2) And you can also use them for <u>linking</u> two parts of a sentence <u>together</u>.

Hillary is a girl <u>who</u> wants a world without soap.

They were chased by a dog <u>which</u> was enormous.

Use '<u>Who</u>' For <u>People</u> And Use '<u>Which</u>' For <u>Things</u>

When you write about <u>people</u> you <u>always</u> need to use '<u>who</u>'.

I have two friends <u>who</u> are in the 'Bloated Eye' contest.

<u>Who</u>'d have thought they'd meet in the final?

But when you're writing about <u>animals</u> or <u>things</u>, you've got to use '<u>which</u>'.

We have two cats <u>which</u> like drinking tea.　<u>Which</u> cat is yours?

They were showing three Bond films <u>which</u> he hadn't seen.

'<u>Who</u>' goes with <u>people</u> and
'<u>which</u>' goes with <u>animals</u> and <u>things</u>.

Things in the desert — sand whiches, perhaps...

'<u>Who</u>' and '<u>which</u>' are incredibly useful little words. The big thing to learn is '<u>who</u>' goes with <u>people</u> and '<u>which</u>' goes with <u>animals</u> and <u>things</u>. Some people act like animals but they still need '<u>who</u>'.

Relationship Words

There are loads of common words you use to show the 'position' of one thing related to another. These are words like 'in', 'out', 'up', 'down', 'on', 'off' and 'behind'.

These Words Tell You Where the Thing Is

1) You need that little word '<u>in</u>' here to say <u>where</u> Mandy is.

> *Mandy is <u>in</u> the wheelie bin.*

2) This time the word '<u>behind</u>' shows <u>where</u> Mandy is in <u>relation</u> to the rubbish.

> *Mandy is <u>behind</u> the rubbish.*

3) Here '<u>under</u>' tells you where Mandy is in <u>relation</u> to the recycling.

> *Mandy's stuck <u>under</u> the recycling.*

Don't Confuse 'In' and 'Into'

These two words are easy to get wrong, but they actually mean <u>different things</u>.

> You need to use '<u>in</u>' to show their <u>position</u>...

> *They are <u>in</u> my bath.*

> *They clambered <u>into</u> my bath.*

> ...but you must use '<u>into</u>' to show they are <u>entering</u> something — they're <u>moving</u> into it.

Remember — '<u>in</u>' means <u>position</u>: '<u>into</u>' means <u>entering</u> something.

She is <u>in</u> the shower.   *She got <u>into</u> the shower.*

= where she is.   = where she's going.

Relationship rules — learn to love your 'in'-laws...

<u>Don't</u> get 'in' and 'into' muddled — '<u>in</u>' is about <u>position</u>, and '<u>into</u>' is about <u>entering</u> something. 'Into' <u>always</u> goes with an <u>action word</u> about a <u>movement</u>, like 'go', 'fall' or 'run'. <u>Learn</u> the difference now.

'To', 'Till' and 'Until'

The common mistakes with 'to', 'till' and 'until' are exceptionally picky ones.
There's a slight difference in meaning which can end up being expensive for your marks.

Watch Out for These Three Troublesome Words

1) 'To', 'till' and 'until' cause nothing but problems unless you learn exactly how to use them.

They ran until the park.   *They ran till the park.*

NO!   2) Both these sentences are wrong.

They ran to the park.

3) This is the right word to use. You've got to use 'to' if you're writing about a place.

I went to school on a sheep.

4) School is a place so you must use 'to'. Don't put 'till' or 'until' by mistake.

You Need 'Till' or 'Until' to Write About Time

= WRONG

You have to use 'until' or 'till' with times.

We waited to eight to start the meal.

We waited until eight to start the meal.

You can't use 'to' here — you'll lose marks.

There's nothing like roast fleas.

Hmmf?

But you can use 'to' together with 'from' in sentences like this.

The chip van is open from 6.30 to 11.00.

 This is also right.   *The chip van is open from 6.30 till 11.00.*

Learn this page — more tills than a supermarket...

'Till', 'until' and 'to' are really handy words that you're forever using in your writing. Make sure you learn the difference between them — you need 'to' for places; 'till', 'until' and 'from...to...' for times.

Revision Summary

Time to take a quick breather before you get started on these wonderful revision questions. Yes, here's a page to test yourself and see what you've learned about all these different words. The main thing is don't cheat by looking back over the section. Try to answer the questions without looking back. It's the only way to find out what you really know. If you get stuck with a question, then go over the pages about that topic when you're finished. Once you've got them straight, try answering the question again. That's the best way to learn this stuff — and that'll definitely help to improve your marks.

1)   What are the four kinds of noun?
2)   Give two examples of each kind of noun.
3)   When do you need to use a plural form of a noun?
4)   Give the plural forms of these words: a) *cat*, b) *horse*, c) *squirrel*.
5)   How do you form the plural of words that end in -y: a) If the letter before -y is a vowel?
      b) If the letter before -y is a consonant?   c) If they are people's names?
6)   What is the plural of 'sheep'?
7)   What is the plural of: a) *fox?* b) *match?* c) *class?*
8)   What is the plural of: a) *tomato?* b) *disco?* c) *shelf?* d) *belief?* e) *life?*
9)   What is the plural of: a) *mouse?* b) *man?* c) *oasis?*
10) What is a pronoun?
11) Which word is the pronoun in this sentence?   *"He went to the park."*
12) When do you need to use 'I', 'you', 'he/she/it', 'we' or 'they'?
13) Write a sentence using 'I'. Then write another using 'they'.
14) When do you use 'me', 'you', 'him/her/it', 'us' or 'them'?
15) Write a sentence using 'her', and then another one using 'us'.
16) When do you use 'mine', 'yours', 'his/hers/its', 'ours', 'theirs'?
17) Write one sentence using 'yours', and another using 'theirs'.
18) What's wrong with this sentence?   *"Me and Eric went to the pictures."*
19) What should you write instead of 'between you and I'?
20) What are the two main ways you use 'who' and 'which'?
21) What's the difference between them?
22) What do you use the words 'in', 'on' or 'behind' for?
23) Give an example sentence using 'in', another one using 'on', and another using 'behind'.
24) What's the difference between 'in' and 'into'?
25) What do you use 'to' for?
26) Give an example sentence using 'to'.
27) What do you use 'till' and 'until' for?
28) Write one sentence using 'till', and another one using 'until'.
29) Write a sentence using the phrase 'from...to...'
30) Learn the ten words below off by heart.
      Make sure you can spell them all perfectly before you move on.

definitely	belief	information	judge	desperate
mostly	thieves	fascinating	awkward	certainly

What a Verb Is

Verbs are boring. There's no way around that, I'm afraid.
Unfortunately, they're things you really have to know about — stick this page deep in your memory.

A Verb is a 'Doing' or 'Being' Word

1) Here's a 'doing' word.

She _eats_ rice for lunch.

2) 'Doing' words tell you what happens in a sentence.

Joe _rides_ to Tibet every day.

3) These are 'being' words.

I _am_ very happy.

Today _is_ a good day.

Words like 'Seem' are also Verbs

Shakespeare's comedies never _seem_ very funny.

The Form of a Verb Tells You When It Was Done

Verbs change form to show if something
was done in the past, in the future or in the present.

I _went_ to school.

= in the past.

I _will go_ to school.

= in the future.

I _go_ to school.

= in the present.

These forms are called tenses.

To do is to be...to be is to do...do be do be do...

This is all stuff you need to know — take your time and make sure you get it clear. Remember — verbs are 'doing' and 'being' words, and they change tense to show when they were done. If that sounds tricky, scribble it down in rough and say it over till it's sunk in. It's really important you do.

Two Kinds of Present Verbs

This _isn't_ hard — you've _used_ these forms _all your life_, but no one's _explained_ them before.
The _present tense_ is about what _happens_ or _is happening_ now. Get this _clear_ before you go on.

You Use Present Verbs to Say What Happens

Fiona _drives_ to work in a tank.

= this is _what_ she _does_.

Some postmen _run_ away from cats.

= this is _what_ they _do_.

You need this ace form for writing about stuff
that's _always true_ or that _keeps on happening_.

You _can't_ fit an elephant in your bath.

= this is _always_ true, unless you've got a massive bath.

The Continuous Present Says What Is Happening

1) For this you need: _am/are/is + verb + -ing_.

The lads _are dancing_ again.

2) This means it's _still_ going on.

I _am sitting_ up a tree.

3) Here I'm _still_ up in the tree.

Learn this now — no time like the present...

Get this straight — the _present_ is about _now_. All that means is you need to use the _-ing form_ to write
about stuff that's _still going on_, and the other form for stuff that's _always true_ or _keeps on happening_.

Forming Present Verbs

The problem with <u>present verbs</u> is that people think they're easy and end up making <u>silly mistakes</u>. There's only <u>one way</u> to avoid that — you'll have to <u>learn</u> how to <u>form</u> them properly.

Most Verbs Follow a Pattern in the Present

The verb '<u>to take</u>' is a great example.

He <u>takes</u> aim...

I take	we take
you take	you take
he takes	
she takes	they take
it takes	

You've got to <u>learn</u> this pattern. Don't forget — <u>only</u> the '<u>he</u>', '<u>she</u>' and '<u>it</u>' forms end in an '<u>s</u>'.

You Need to Memorize these Tricky Forms too

VERB	I	YOU	HE	SHE	IT	WE	YOU	THEY
to be	am	are	is	is	is	are	are	are
to do	do	do	does	does	does	do	do	do
to have	have	have	has	has	has	have	have	have
to fly	fly	fly	flies	flies	flies	fly	fly	fly
to go	go	go	goes	goes	goes	go	go	go

It <u>flies</u>!

These are <u>dead common forms</u>. People get them <u>wrong</u> by being careless. They <u>won't</u> be a nightmare as long as you <u>learn</u> them all — especially how to <u>spell</u> them.

Tricky presents — like Mum's birthday all over...

Plenty to be getting on with here. The way to <u>avoid</u> silly mistakes with <u>present verbs</u> is <u>learn</u> the <u>pattern</u> of 'to take'. Then you've absolutely got to learn the table of <u>tricky forms</u>. There are loads of <u>other verbs</u> that <u>don't follow</u> the pattern, but these are the <u>big ones</u> — so make sure you <u>scribble</u> them down in rough and get them <u>learned</u>. Start with the verb '<u>to be</u>' — it's the <u>key</u>.

PRESENT PARTICIPLES

Forming -ing Verbs

This is an important bit — the <u>-ing form</u> in the present is only <u>part</u> of the verb.
You've got to use a <u>helping verb</u> with it — 'am', 'is' or 'are'.

-ing Verbs Show Something is Continuing to Happen

1) This form shows the action is <u>continuing</u>.

He <u>is chasing</u> the alien.

He <u>chases</u> the alien.

2) The other present form stresses <u>what</u> the action is.

The -ing Verb Needs a Helping Verb

The helping verb you need here is '<u>to be</u>'.
Remember <u>am/is/are</u> from the last page.

I am screaming	**We** are screaming
You are screaming	**You** are screaming
He is screaming	
She is screaming	**They** are screaming
It is screaming	

Here's the <u>helping verb</u>.

I <u>am</u> going home.

We <u>are</u> feeling ill.

And this is the <u>helping verb</u> here.

Learn the Rule — In the Present add am/is/are + -ing

Igor <u>is</u> hiding under this example.

It's simple really —
the action's <u>still continuing</u>.

How to spell -ing — a spelling problem...

That's more like it — a nice <u>easy rule</u> to learn here. Don't forget — you need to use am/is/are +
verb + -ing. It's another one of those forms that you use all the time anyway. This page is for
<u>checking</u> that you're using it the right way — it shows the action is <u>still going on</u> in the present.

How to Spell -ing Words

All the stuff about -ing words has been <u>pretty easy</u> so far — but here's where it gets <u>tough</u>. They're a <u>nightmare</u> to spell correctly. That means you'll have to <u>learn</u> these rules <u>right now</u>.

Watch Out for Verbs like 'Flap', 'Hit' and 'Shop'

1) Here you need to <u>double</u> the '<u>t</u>' and then <u>add</u> -ing.

Brian keeps hit<u>ting</u> the ball for six.

2) This time you've got to add an <u>extra 'p'</u> before the -ing.

The bat is flap<u>ping</u> its wings.

3) 'Hit' and 'flap' both have a <u>short vowel sound</u> — 'i', 'a'. They also <u>end</u> in a <u>consonant</u> — 't' and 'p'.

When you add -ing to verbs like this, you've got to stick on <u>another consonant</u>.

shop<u>p</u>ing   *put<u>t</u>ing*

Don't forget — <u>vowels</u> are the letters a, e, i, o, u. All the other letters are called <u>consonants</u>.

You Just Add -ing to Verbs Like 'Keep' or 'Eat'

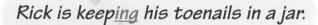
This verb's got a <u>long vowel sound</u> — 'ee'.

Rick is keep<u>ing</u> his toenails in a jar.

You <u>only</u> need <u>-ing</u> to spell it properly.

She is eat<u>ing</u>.

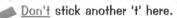
<u>Don't</u> stick another 't' here.

Most Long Verbs follow these Rules too...

This one follows the <u>first rule</u>...

She is begin<u>n</u>ing to dance.

...but this one <u>doesn't</u> — there's only <u>one</u> 'r' here.

You are offe<u>r</u>ing me chocolate.

Watch out for the ones that <u>don't</u> — and <u>learn</u> them.

More on Spelling -ing Words

There's more, I'm afraid — but believe me, <u>learning</u> these rules will seriously <u>improve</u> your spelling. Don't forget that it's the <u>little mistakes</u> in your work that end up <u>costing</u> you the <u>most marks</u>.

Stick on an -ing with These Two Kinds of Verb

1) Verbs ending in Two Vowels

He is s<u>ee</u>ing her tomorrow.

2) Verbs ending in Two Consonants

He is wa<u>lk</u>ing on the rope,
but she is sti<u>ck</u>ing to the path.

Chop off Silent 'e' Endings Before You Add -ing

You've got to <u>chop off</u> the 'e' from 'guide'.

The dog is <u>guiding</u> us out of danger.

Here you need to <u>chop</u> the 'e' off 'take'.

You are <u>taking</u> us for a ride.

Always <u>chop off</u> the '<u>-e</u>' before '<u>-ing</u>'.
It's a <u>whopper</u> of a mistake if you don't.

They are <u>mistaking</u> me for Elvis again.

<u>No</u> 'e' here either.

How do you pronounce a silent 'e' —   ...

Spelling mistakes are a <u>massive turn off</u> — the examiners think "low marks" straight away.
These <u>-ing words</u> are a real killer. Your best bet is to <u>learn</u> these <u>rules</u>. Remember — verbs with <u>long vowel sounds</u> like 'ee', 'ea', 'oo' always just <u>add -ing</u>. The <u>biggest mistake</u> people make is with <u>silent 'e's</u> — it'll really drag your marks down. Learn this — if the 'e' is silent, <u>cut it out</u> before -ing.

Two More Uses for '-ing' Words

This is boring but <u>important</u> — you use '-ing' words in some <u>other ways</u> too.
The good news is you <u>don't</u> need to worry about any of the <u>technical stuff</u>.
You've <u>just</u> got to make sure you can <u>use</u> these forms when you're <u>writing</u> — so get learning now.

You Can Use '-ing' Words as Nouns too

1) There's <u>no</u> am/is/are here — the -ing word <u>isn't</u> a verb here.

I hate <u>shopping</u>.

2) <u>This</u> word's the verb.

<u>Stealing</u> is wrong.

3) Same again — the -ing word is the <u>main noun</u>; the verb is '<u>is</u>'.

<u>Laughing</u> in class can get you into trouble.

SILENCE!

4) It really <u>isn't</u> difficult — you say things like this <u>all the time</u>.

Don't forget — the <u>spelling rules</u> are still the <u>same</u>.

You Use Some '-ing' Words in Descriptions

She flew through the air like a <u>shooting</u> star.

These are <u>describing words</u>.

Look out below!

The <u>squeaking</u> mouse ran under the <u>flying</u> carpet.

Describing words like these make the sentences
<u>more exciting</u> to read — and pick up <u>more marks</u>.

Nouns & descriptions — with the '-ing' crowd...

This stuff about '-ing' words may seem pretty <u>dull</u> — but they can be a <u>major headache</u> if you don't
know all the ins and outs. This page is about getting them <u>clear</u> in your mind for your <u>written work</u>.
If you <u>haven't</u> learned the <u>spelling rules</u>, go over them. There's more about <u>describing words</u> on P.49.

Was/Were & '-ing' Words

We're still <u>not finished</u> with '-ing' words yet, I'm afraid. You <u>can't</u> get away from them that easily. They've got another <u>big job</u> with <u>verbs</u> — only this time it's in the <u>past</u> not the present.

Was/Were + Verb + '-ing' = Continuing in the Past

1) This happened in the <u>past</u>...

I <u>was going</u> to the haunted cinema.

2) ...but it was <u>continuing</u> to happen at that time.

It <u>was raining</u> for the whole journey.

3) Typical — the rain was <u>still going on</u>.

We <u>were fishing</u> for pike all day.

4) The fishing was <u>continuing</u> for the <u>whole day</u>.

Instead of am/is/are, you've got to stick
'<u>was</u>' or '<u>were</u>' in front of the '-<u>ing</u>' word in the <u>past</u>.

WAS Goes with I, He/She/It; WERE Goes with We, You, They

She <u>was leaving</u> town.

They <u>were waving</u> good-bye.

Remember — these are <u>past</u>
actions that <u>went on</u> for some time.

The past — it isn't what it used to be...

This is an <u>easy place</u> to start learning about <u>verbs</u> in the <u>past</u>. These forms are really simple — was/were + '-ing' verb. Even better — the '-ing' words still follow the <u>same spelling rules</u>, so if you've learned them, you <u>won't</u> have <u>any</u> problems. If not, go back to P.15 and get them <u>learned</u> right now. And don't forget — was/were + verb + 'ing' = things <u>still happening</u> in the <u>past</u>.

Verbs in the Past

Sadly, '-ing' words <u>aren't</u> the end of the past tense story — they're only the <u>beginning</u>.
The <u>biggest problem</u> with the past is making sure you <u>don't</u> get the different forms <u>confused</u>.
The easy way to <u>avoid</u> that is by <u>learning</u> the <u>three key past forms</u>.

Learn *these* Three Key Past Forms

① I <u>invented</u> a magic potion.

This one's about a <u>single action</u> that happened <u>once</u> in the past and was <u>finished</u>. It's the ordinary form.

② I <u>have invented</u> a magic potion.

You've got to use this one to talk about something that <u>happened</u> and was <u>finished</u> in the <u>recent past</u>.

③ I <u>was inventing</u> a magic potion.

And here's the one from the last page. The inventing was <u>still happening</u> at the time. It <u>wasn't finished</u> then.

<u>You</u> <u>Must Learn</u> <u>the</u> <u>Difference</u> <u>between</u> these Forms

More easy bits — this is just to <u>make sure</u> you know the <u>difference</u> between them.
You've got to use them the <u>right way</u> in your writing. It's the only way to <u>boost</u> your marks.

I learned.	I have learnt.	I was learning.
= FINISHED.	= RECENTLY FINISHED.	= NOT FINISHED.

Italian history — it happened in the past-a...

It all sounds very complicated, but it <u>isn't</u> really. All you <u>need</u> to know is that <u>different past tense</u> forms have <u>different meanings</u>. You'll need to <u>use</u> these forms a lot in your writing — especially if you're writing <u>stories</u>. The trick is to remember that <u>each form</u> means something slightly different.

THE SIMPLE PAST TENSE	

Forming the Ordinary Past

This is where you <u>need</u> to keep your eyes open. The next bit's deadly boring.
People are <u>always</u> getting these verbs in a <u>tangle</u>. You need to <u>learn</u> this page to <u>stay out</u> of trouble.

1) <u>Loads</u> of Verbs Add '-ed' in the Past

He work<u>ed</u>.   You crack<u>ed</u> a vase.   They stay<u>ed</u>.

2) <u>Some</u> Verbs Add '-t' Instead

Ellie learn<u>t</u> nothing.   Tom leap<u>t</u> towards the rhino.

3) <u>Verbs</u> With 'ee' in the Middle

<u>Lose</u> one 'e' and stick a '<u>-t</u>' on the end.

We wep<u>t</u> for joy.   He slep<u>t</u> soundly.   United kep<u>t</u> going.

4) <u>Ten</u> Mega Important Verbs You Need to Learn

These ones are <u>dead common</u> — you'll <u>need them</u> all the time when you're <u>writing</u>.
<u>Scribble</u> them down and <u>learn</u> them — make sure you get all the <u>spellings</u> crystal clear.

I <u>thought</u> she'd never catch the mega-ball.

do → <u>did</u>	be → <u>was/were</u>
have → <u>had</u>	go → <u>went</u>
see → <u>saw</u>	take → <u>took</u>
steal → <u>stole</u>	catch → <u>caught</u>
think → <u>thought</u>	fight → <u>fought</u>

I <u>caught</u> it!

Retired goalkeepers — goalkepters, perhaps...

The ordinary past sounds <u>incredibly yawnsome</u>, I know. The thing is, it's one of those places where you can <u>lose</u> easy marks for <u>silly mistakes</u>. If you can get this page <u>learnt</u>, you're in with a <u>chance</u>.

The Past Tense with 'Have'

There's <u>another way</u> to talk about something that happened in the <u>past</u>.
You put it together by adding '<u>has</u>' or '<u>have</u>' to a special past form.

You Need to Use this Past Tense for Two Things

> I <u>have lost</u> sixteen grams.

1) You're saying that the 'losing' happened <u>recently</u> but it's <u>finished</u> now.

> She <u>has loved</u> him for years.

2) Here you're saying that the 'loving' has been <u>going on</u> for a <u>period</u> of time.

GROAN!

> For 'I', 'You', 'We' and 'They' <u>always</u> use '<u>have</u>'.
> For 'He', 'She' and 'It' you've <u>got</u> to use '<u>has</u>'.

You Must Learn these Tricky Common Ones

to do	have/has done	to go	have/has gone
to be	have/has been	to begin	have/has begun
to have	have/has had	to write	have/has written
to take	have/has taken	to steal	have/has stolen
to eat	have/has eaten	to hide	have/has hidden

Sometimes the <u>second bit</u> of these verb forms looks the <u>same</u> as the ordinary past —
but really it <u>isn't</u>. Don't get confused — scribble down the <u>common forms</u> and <u>learn</u> them.

> She <u>has slept</u> well.   She <u>slept</u> well.

These two <u>look</u> the same but they <u>aren't</u>. <u>Don't</u> get confused.

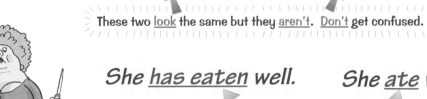

> She <u>has eaten</u> well.   She <u>ate</u> well.

These two are completely <u>different</u> — so <u>don't</u> put 'eaten' when you <u>mean</u> 'ate'.

The Big Mistake with 'Have'

This is the <u>crucial bit</u>. It's where you can <u>drop</u> loads of <u>marks</u> if you're not careful.

Don't Use this Tense Without 'Have' or 'Has'

I <u>been</u> flying. = **WRONG**

You've <u>got</u> to use '<u>have</u>' or '<u>has</u>' with 'been'.

I <u>have</u> been flying. = **RIGHT**

Never Write 'Done' without 'Have' or 'Has'
— And Don't Use it When You Mean 'Did'

1) This is <u>completely</u> wrong.

*I **done** my science homework.*

2) You're <u>confusing</u> two <u>different</u> forms — '<u>did</u>' and '<u>have done</u>'.

<u>I did</u> my science homework.   **OR**   *<u>I have done</u> my science homework.*

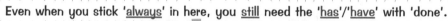

You can <u>only</u> write '<u>I did</u>' or '<u>I have done</u>'.
<u>Never</u> put 'I done'.

You Can Add Extra Words But You Still Need 'Has' or 'Have'

Even when you stick '<u>always</u>' in here, you <u>still</u> need the '<u>has</u>'/'have' with 'done'.

They <u>have</u> always <u>done</u> DIY.

It's the same for <u>any</u> verb <u>like</u> 'done' — you <u>must</u> put in '<u>have</u>' or '<u>has</u>'.

We <u>have</u> recently <u>been</u> buying hammers.

Learn grammar on the farm — 'I have dung'...

Phew — it all seems a bit <u>tricky</u>. The <u>main thing</u> to remember is <u>every time</u> you use this past tense you've got to stick '<u>have</u>' or '<u>has</u>' on the front. And <u>never</u> put '<u>done</u>' when you mean '<u>did</u>'.

SECTION TWO — VERBS

The Other Big Mistake with 'Have'

You're not out of the woods yet — there's another <u>whopping mistake</u> you've got to <u>watch out for</u>.

Don't __Write Sentences Like__ These

What wouldst thou get if thou cross'd an elephant with a mouse?

Big holes in thy skirting board.

He <u>couldn't of</u> gone to the match.   = WRONG

Shakespeare <u>would of</u> made an awful stand-up comic.

<u>Don't</u> write things like this.

You Need to Use 'Have' NOT 'of'

CREAK! CRACK!

Ow, my back!

1) Here's what it <u>should</u> say.

He couldn't <u>have</u> gone to the match.

2) You must use '<u>could have gone</u>' — 'could of gone' <u>doesn't</u> exist.

Shakespeare would <u>have</u> made an awful stand-up comic.

3) '<u>Would have made</u>' is the phrase you need here — 'would of made' is totally <u>wrong</u>.

> <u>Never</u> write 'might of', 'could of', 'should of', 'would of' in your work.
> You've got to use '<u>might have</u>', '<u>could have</u>', '<u>should have</u>', '<u>would have</u>'.

The Short Form of 'Could Have' is 'Could've'

This is where you can easily get <u>muddled</u> — 'could've' sounds a <u>lot</u> like 'could of'.
But <u>don't forget</u> — 'could of' is <u>wrong</u>. You must use '<u>could have</u>' in your writing work.

I could <u>have</u> told you that.

Mistakes with 'have' — I could've been had...

Another <u>big one</u> to watch out for. It's far too <u>easy</u> to write 'could of', 'should of', 'might of' or 'would of' <u>by mistake</u>. Whatever you do, <u>don't</u> make that mistake — you need '<u>have</u>' not 'of'.

VERBS OF ABILITY & POSSIBILITY

Can, May and Might

'Can', 'may' and 'might' are three annoying little verbs that people always get confused.
They're all to do with possibilities and being able to do things. Make sure you learn the differences.

You Must Use 'Can' for Being Able to Do Something

He delivers pizza so he _can_ ride his bike all day.

= he is able to do it.

= I am physically able to do it.

I _can_ stand on my head for five minutes.

Use 'May' for Asking Permission...

Don't use 'can' when you mean 'may'.

Can I go to the toilet?

= am I able to go?

May I go to the toilet?

= am I allowed to go?

...and for Strong Possibilities

I _may_ be going to the cinema tomorrow.

This means it's very likely to happen.

You Need 'Might' if it's an Unlikely Possibility

My flying machine _might_ take off one day.

It's possible but I really don't think it'll happen.

May — a permissive month, perhaps...

These three words cause all sorts of trouble if you don't use them properly. This is the time to learn
what they mean once and for all. Remember — can means 'being able', may is used for permission
and strong possibilities, might is used for unlikely possibilities. Sounds alright — now learn them.

Don't and Doesn't

How often do you hear people say things like 'He don't care'...
Well, the bad news is they're wrong. It's all to do with a big muddle over 'don't' and 'doesn't'.

Learn _This Now:_

> 'Don't' is short for 'do not'.
> 'Doesn't' is short for 'does not'.

1) Look at this sentence. Think about the long form.

It _don't_ work properly. = WRONG

2) 'It do not work' sounds horrible.
   This can't be right — you'll need 'doesn't' instead.

It _doesn't_ work properly.

3) Now look at this one.

He _doesn't_ know it but they _don't_ bounce.

4) 'He does not know' = right; and 'they do not bounce' = right. This sentence is fine.

You've Got to Use 'Doesn't' with 'He', 'She' and 'It'

> Never use 'don't' with
> 'he', 'she' or 'it'.

Remember the present tense forms on P.13 —
I do, you do, he/she/it does, we do, you do, they do.

He _doesn't_ change the bulb often.

= he/she/it does + not.

I _don't_ think he knows how.

= I do + not.

You _don't_ do it like that.

= you do + not.

A messy war film with 'don't' — 'The Dirty Doesn't'...

'Don't' and 'doesn't' are two words you use all the time. That makes it harder if you've been using them wrongly. The main thing to remember is you must use 'doesn't' with 'he', 'she' and 'it'. Never use 'don't' with these ones — just with 'I', 'you', 'we' and 'they'. Learn this page right now.

CONSISTENCY OF TENSES

Staying in the Right Tense

This is the biggest mistake you need to avoid with verbs.
Make sure you've learnt all the different tense forms in this section before you look at this page.

Don't Change Tenses in Your Writing By Mistake

This is past tense.

Another past verb.

> As they tried to get the sail up, they could hear distant splashes. Suddenly, they see a canoe.

This one's wrong — it's present when it should be past.

You Must Only Use Past Verbs in Past Writing

If you start writing in the past, you've got to stay in the past.

> Everything was silent. John and I crouched behind the rock.
> We had been waiting for almost three hours in the hot sun.
> Nothing around us was moving. Until the trees rustled behind me.

All the verbs here are past forms — you can tell exactly what's going on.

Be consistent — don't muddle your tenses.
Stay in one tense so it's clear what's going on.

Be Especially Careful with the Present

1) You need the present for literature essays.

NO!

> Even though Piggy is annoying, Ralph realised he is often right.

I know they're here somewhere...

2) Don't mix past and present forms by mistake.

> Even though Piggy is annoying, Ralph realises he is often right.

3) Much better — you really bring the description to life by using the present.

Consistency of tenses — a sticky business...

Sticking to the same tense — it sounds so simple. But when you're writing in a hurry, it's easy to put the wrong one down without thinking. Learn this page and remember your tenses when you write.

Revision Summary

Plenty to be getting on with here. Verbs cause all sorts of problems in people's writing. The thing is, most of the mistakes can be avoided. You just need to get your tenses straight and learn the really nasty muddles to watch out for. Sounds simple enough — but now it's time to find out how much you've really learned. It's question time again — and don't even think about cheating. It's not worth it. If you want to get a decent grade, you need to put the effort in. That's all it comes down to.

1) What is a verb?
2) What does the tense of a verb tell you?
3) Give two sentences in the present tense.
4) Write down all of the present tense forms of the verb 'to be'.
5) Write down all the present tense forms of the verb 'to make'.
6) What does the -ing form in the present show?
7) Give two sentences using -ing forms in the present tense.
8) Give the -ing form of the following words. Make sure you spell them correctly:
   a) *sit*, b) *sleep*, c) *shop*, d) *begin*, e) *offer*, f) *flee*, g) *stick*, h) *take*.
9) Write two sentences where you use -ing words as nouns instead of verbs.
10) Write two sentences where you use -ing words for descriptions.
11) Give two sentences using -ing words with 'was' and 'were'.
12) When do you need to use 'was' and when do you need to use 'were'?
13) What are the three key past forms? Give an example of each kind.
14) What is the difference between these forms?
15) Give the ordinary past form of these verbs: a) *sleep*, b) *leap*, c) *walk*, d) *do*.
16) Write a sentence using the verb 'had', and a sentence using the word 'went'.
17) Give two sentences which use 'have' or 'has' with a past form.
18) What is the 'have'/'has' form of: a) *'to do'?* b) *'to take'?* c) *'to eat'?* d) *'to steal'?*
19) What should you never forget when you use the 'have' form?
20) What's the difference between 'did' and 'done'?
21) What's wrong with writing 'He could of done it.' ?
22) What's the short form of 'could have'?
23) What's the difference between 'can', 'may' and 'might'?
24) Write a sentence using 'can', one using 'may' and one using 'might'.
25) What is 'don't' short for? What is 'doesn't' short for?
26) Give a sentence using 'don't' and one using 'doesn't'.
27) Which of the two should you always use with 'he', 'she' or 'it'?
28) What's the biggest mistake you need to avoid with verbs?
29) When should you be especially careful?
30) Learn these ten words off by heart — and make sure you can spell them too.

become	becoming	character	scene	because
unnecessary	panic	panicked	accurate	vicious

Watch out for that 'k' in panicked.

| REVISING CAPITALS | *Capital Letters* |

Capital letters seem such an obvious thing. Well think again.
Start forgetting them too often when you write, and you could drop down one whole grade.
That's deadly serious — so make sure you learn this stuff really well.

Remember *the Capitals at the* Start *of Sentences*

1) Every sentence starts with a capital letter.

Tomorrow I'll strap a rocket to my bike and fly off into space.

2) Only a few special words have a capital in the middle of a sentence.

Harry met his mate Bert in Swansea and Had beetroot pizzas.

NO! Don't stick extra capitals in.
You'll just lose marks.

THE BIG THING is be careful — it's not enough to know where to put capitals.
You've got to make them dead obvious when you write them.

Make Your Capitals *Twice as Big as Your* Small Letters

Cc Oo Ss Uu Vv

(It's the same with w, x, z, p.)

Size is important

Watch out though — these ones are all the same size.
Just make sure the letters are obviously different shapes.

Ll Kk Ff

Big capitals — I've heard London's massive...

Capital letters really are something you don't want to lose marks for — that'd just be a waste. Don't forget — every sentence starts with a capital, and when you write capitals they've got to be clear.

Six Places You Need Capitals

Capital letters are a funny bunch — they turn up in <u>all sorts</u> of places.
Save yourself any problems by learning <u>exactly</u> when you <u>need</u> a capital — right here, right now.

1) **People's** Names **and** Titles

My name's Cedrico Obidiah Thribblewort. Got a problem with that?

Always write people's names with a <u>capital letter</u>.
People's titles have a capital too — Mr, Mrs, Ms, Dr...

Ms Lisa Brown

2) **Names of** Towns **and** Places

Think of the name of your <u>home town</u>.
You'd always write that with a <u>capital letter</u>.

Birmingham

3) **Things to Do with** Countries

English

Nationalities.

I am <u>F</u>rench. I come from <u>F</u>rance. I speak <u>F</u>rench.

Languages.

Countries.

the Ministry of Transport

4) **Names of** Companies **and** Organisations

Ace Incorporated Free can of fishy pop! Offer ends Thursday 18th April.

Thursday

August

5) Days **of the Week**

Bob eats cabbage cake on <u>M</u>onday and <u>T</u>uesday.

6) Months **of the Year**

<u>M</u>arch and <u>A</u>pril are good months for wrestling snakes.

The Capital of Wales — that's just 'W'...

Time to get this little lot <u>learned</u> — I know it seems a bit too easy, but you still <u>need</u> to know it.
There's really <u>no excuse</u> for losing <u>any marks</u> for your capital letters — so <u>make sure</u> you don't.

EXCLAMATION MARKS

Exclamation Marks

Exclamation marks are cool — they make things jump out of the page at you, like this!

Exclamation Marks are like STRONG Full Stops

You'll need these little beggars when a sentence shows strong feelings.

!

Go away!

Stop it!

I've won £1000!

I'm over here!

It was brilliant!

Here's where you use them:

1) if the sentence is a command.

2) when someone's shouting.

3) to show surprise or anger.

Moo!

REMEMBER — the exclamation mark replaces the full stop. Don't put a full stop in as well.

Don't Use Exclamation Marks All the Time

We couldn't hear anything!
Taking a deep breath, Jack
opened the door! We gasped in
horror at the same moment!
The ducks had escaped!

NO! Far too many exclamations here.

You can't tell which bit is supposed to jump out at you.

Never Use More Than One '!' in One Sentence

Don't do this — it's wrong.

That's loads better.

Ouch!!!

Only use one!

Retired shellfish country — ex-clam-nation...

There are two big mistakes people always make with exclamation marks — they forget to put them in, or they stick in far too many. Start by learning the three uses — just think of strong feelings.

Question Marks

The question mark is another sneaky one that's easy to mess up when you're writing in a hurry. Think of it as a confused full stop — it's always waiting for an answer.

Question Marks Go at the End of Questions

Any sentence asking a question must end with a QUESTION MARK instead of a full stop.

Have you seen a rhino bungee jump?

Are these my apples or yours?

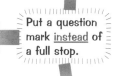
Put a question mark instead of a full stop.

Where can I find more chairs?

All proper questions in your writing need a '?'
Don't miss any out and you won't miss out on the marks.

If It Isn't Really a Question — There's No '?'

Watch out — some sentences tell you about a question, but don't actually ask one.

Herman wondered where he could find more chairs.

These sentences aren't asking questions...

...and there's no question mark here.

She asked me how many bakers fit in a 2CV.

Question marks — they're confused full stops...

The really tricky part about question marks is working out what is a question and what isn't.
Remember — a sentence which is actually asking for an answer definitely must have a question mark.

Commas

Hmm — <u>commas</u> are one of those annoying things you're really <u>meant</u> to know about.
The problem is, they're a real <u>tough cookie</u> to get right.
The <u>only way</u> to do it is by <u>learning</u> all of this stuff, I'm afraid. So start <u>right now</u>.

Commas break up lists, add ideas and keep sentences clear.

I make
it clear.

Commas Break Things Up in Lists

I love ice cream cake sandwiches and chips.

 **EH?**

1) <u>Without</u> commas, you <u>can't tell</u> what this is about.

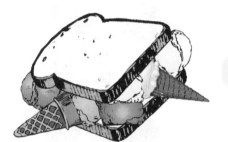

I love ice cream, cake, sandwiches and chips.

2) Phew — <u>now</u> it's clear. I was starting to wonder
what 'ice cream cake sandwiches' were like.

Don't forget — when you write a list,
put a comma after each thing... except the last two.

George Michael?

Michael Owen?

Sounds like some pretty famous best mates.

George Michael Owen and Dave are my best mates.

George, Michael, Owen and Dave are my best mates.

Aha — just your normal school mates then.

Use an 'And' or an 'Or' with the Last Two Things

<u>Instead</u> of a comma, put '<u>and</u>' or '<u>or</u>'
between the <u>last two things</u>.

Should I dye my hair green, blue, pink <u>or</u> purple?

Commas are like fast dogs — quick paws...

Without commas, your sentences <u>won't</u> be clear. This is dead important for writing <u>lists</u> — you'll
just sound really <u>confused</u>. Remember — you need a comma <u>after</u> every item <u>except</u> the <u>last two</u>.

Commas Make the Meaning Clear

Get this straight now — commas help to make things <u>clear</u>.
They're a great way to <u>break up</u> long sentences — especially the ones with <u>more than one</u> point.

Some Sentences Have More than One Point

Here's <u>one point</u>.

And here's the <u>other</u> one.

Bruce told her to be quiet, but she started to growl.

Quiet!

Each action is in a <u>separate bit</u> of the sentence — this comma makes it <u>clear</u>.

Grrr!

The Comma Shows there are Two Clear Points

1) This is <u>one point</u> of the sentence.

2) Here's the <u>other point</u>.

Tom began to sing, and I decided to study on my own.

3) The <u>comma</u> makes the two points <u>clear</u>.

These clear points could just as easily be written <u>separately</u>...

Tom began to sing.   I decided to study on my own.

...but <u>long sentences</u> with commas in the <u>right place</u> are real <u>mark winners</u>.

REMEMBER:
You've got to stick a comma in sentences with two clear points.

The invisible man — he made things clear ...

This is one that people are always <u>getting wrong</u> — don't forget, you need a <u>comma</u> to make things <u>clear</u>. You need to put it somewhere <u>between</u> the two <u>actions</u> — that'll <u>separate</u> them properly.

Commas for Extra Information

Commas really are useful little blighters — remember, they make your writing <u>clearer</u>.
You're bound to pick up <u>extra marks</u> for using them — just as long as you do it <u>properly</u>.

You Need Commas for Adding Stuff to Sentences

The squirrel pounced on the giraffe.

This is a <u>simple sentence</u> that needs some serious <u>livening up</u>
— the easy way to do that is <u>add</u> an <u>extra bit</u>.

With a squeak, the squirrel pounced on the giraffe.

When you stick an <u>extra bit</u> in,
you need a <u>comma</u> to keep it
<u>separate</u> from the main sentence.

He gave everyone a painting, including me.

You've got to stick this comma in to make the sentence
<u>clearer</u> — otherwise it'd sound like <u>I</u> was <u>in</u> the painting.

Sometimes the Extra Bit Goes in the Middle

The twins, who had their blue wigs on, were eating grass.

This example's got <u>two commas</u>
— they're kind of like brackets.

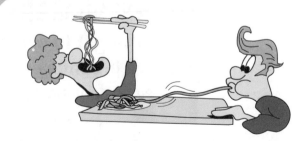

Stick in an extra bit — you know the drill...

Sticking <u>extra information</u> in your sentences makes them loads more <u>interesting</u> to read. Make
sure you <u>don't forget</u> the <u>commas</u> around the extra bit. Start by <u>learning</u> these examples right now.

Dashes

Dashes are those dinky single lines you use to <u>break up</u> sentences — like this.
They're a much <u>stronger break</u> than a comma — they make the reader <u>pause</u> and take a <u>breath</u>.

Use <u>Dashes</u> to <u>Link</u> Two Ideas in <u>One Sentence</u>

Mandy is a famous racing driver — she has won lots of races.

This <u>second bit</u> tells you <u>more</u> about the first.

The Beetles were a great band — they could all sing.

This dash tells you the two ideas <u>go together</u>.

<u>Don't forget</u> — you've got to leave a <u>space</u> either side of the dash.

Dung, Paul, Scarab and Rhino

Dashes Turn <u>Long Sentences</u> into <u>Big Mark Winners</u>

Some sentences get so <u>long</u> that commas <u>aren't</u> enough —
you need <u>dashes</u> to keep them <u>clear</u>.

The dashes make this sentence a lot <u>easier</u> to read.

Oops!

The wind blew and the ship was tossed onto the rocks — the lighthouse had failed — and the cruel sea began to seep into the battered hull.

They're being used <u>like brackets</u> here — just to <u>add in</u> some extra information.

No time for a comma — must dash...

Get this clear — dashes are <u>great</u> for <u>long sentences</u>. They make a <u>clearer break</u> than a comma — but <u>don't</u> use them all the time. The <u>secret</u> with sentences is to have a mix of <u>short</u> and <u>long</u> ones in your writing. Sounds obvious, I know, but most people try to write <u>too many</u> long ones. The thing about <u>dashes</u> is you've got to use them <u>sparingly</u>. Don't stick them in all the time.

Apostrophes and Owning Things

This is really important — apostrophes are something <u>everybody</u> gets wrong.
Get this stuff <u>learned</u> now and you'll save yourself some <u>big marks</u>.

You've Got to Add <u>'s</u> to Show <u>Who Owns</u> Something

Ravi<u>'s</u> pets don't eat much.　　= The pets <u>belong</u> to Ravi.

Trisha<u>'s</u> dog is less scary now.

The dog <u>belongs</u> to Trisha.

Remember — when you're writing about <u>belonging</u>,
add an <u>apostrophe</u> +"<u>s</u>" to the <u>name</u> of the <u>owner</u>.

Some Tricky Names <u>Already</u> End in "s"

Just stick on your apostrophe...　　　...or add apostrophe + "s".

Jesus' disciples　　　St James's park

For <u>Groups</u> of People or Things...

1) If it <u>already</u> ends in <u>s</u>,
stick an <u>apostrophe</u> on the <u>end</u>.

They found the killer <u>eels'</u> lair during
the <u>men's</u> underwater race.

2) Words like <u>men</u>, <u>women</u> and <u>mice</u> follow the normal rule.

I'm a fish agnostic — I don't believe in cod...

It doesn't get much simpler than this. You use apostrophe + s <u>unless</u> it's a <u>word</u> that ends in <u>s</u>.
Life couldn't be quite <u>that</u> simple of course, there are those pesky <u>tricky names</u> that need learning.

Apostrophes and Missing Letters

This is the other thing you'll need <u>apostrophes</u> for — making short forms, like <u>he's</u> instead of <u>he is</u>. You've got to <u>stick</u> in an apostrophe to show there's a letter <u>missing</u>.

We're is the Short Form of We Are

<u>We're</u> is a smashing word you use all the time — but really it's a <u>short form</u> of <u>we are</u>. When you write it, you've got to put an <u>apostrophe</u> instead of the 'a'.

I cut out the 'a'!

Put me here to show something's missing.

we're

<u>We're</u> not sheep, <u>we're</u> goats.

<u>We're</u> going to land on Mars.

Learn these Forms — They Must Have Apostrophes

1) These words are <u>just like</u> we're.

2) They need an <u>apostrophe</u> because they've all got <u>missing letters</u>.

I'm	———	I am
I won't	———	I will not
I'd	———	I would
I'd	———	I had
I've	———	I have

they're	———	they are
who's	———	who is
don't	———	do not
doesn't	———	does not
can't	———	can not

<u>Who's</u> driving the van?

I <u>can't</u> see what I'm doing.

WARNING — Don't Use Apostrophes for Anything Else

NO!

Fresh brown banana<u>'s</u>, 2p for 5.

This is wrong — it'll <u>lose</u> you marks. <u>Never</u> use an apostrophe for plurals.

Short forms — we're not the same as we were...

This is the bit that really causes <u>problems</u>. You've got to <u>remember</u> to put in your <u>apostrophes</u> — or you can kiss goodbye to a lot of marks. Make sure you <u>learn</u> the table on this page <u>right away</u>.

IT'S AND ITS — Don't Confuse It's and Its

These two scoundrels cause <u>more problems</u> than <u>anything else</u> in English grammar.
I reckon they were <u>invented</u> to make trouble — but you can put a stop to it by <u>learning</u> this page.

It's Means 'it is' or 'it has'

<u>It is</u> looking for a snack. → <u>It's</u> looking for a snack.

The apostrophes show a letter has been <u>left out</u>.

<u>It has</u> been a wild and stormy day.

<u>It's</u> been a wild and stormy day.

Its is Like His or Hers — It Doesn't
Follow the Apostrophe Rule

Its = something <u>belongs</u> to <u>it</u>.

You <u>don't</u> use an apostrophe with his or hers so <u>don't</u> use one with its.

Have you fed the dog <u>its</u> dinner?

IS JUST LIKE

Have you fed Rover <u>his</u> dinner?

There <u>aren't</u> any letters missing — you <u>don't need</u> an apostrophe.

Stop and Think — it's or its

1) You <u>must</u> have an apostrophe if you mean <u>it has</u> or <u>it is</u>.
2) <u>Don't</u> use an apostrophe when something <u>belongs</u> to <u>it</u>.

I hate the apostrophe — it's had its day...

There's nothing for it — you've just got to <u>learn</u> these little jokers. Every time you write them down, <u>think</u> what you're saying. Remember — it has or it is give you <u>it's</u>; but <u>its</u> is like his or hers.

Speech Marks

Here's something else that's pretty tough — <u>where</u> and <u>when</u> to put in <u>speech marks</u>.
Just remember — speech marks do <u>exactly</u> what their name says.

Speech Marks *Show Someone's* Actually Speaking

Put us at the start of the speech.

We go at the end.

"You're going to lose that pretty hat," said Bob.

These are the words Bob <u>said</u> — they go in the <u>speech marks</u>.

You're going to lose that pretty hat.

Make Sure the Speech Marks *are at* Both Ends

WRONG! This <u>isn't clear</u> without the speech marks.

I won't lose Bill said.

Loads better — you can see <u>which</u> bit was <u>said</u>.

"I won't lose," Bill said.

Always put <u>speech marks</u> around words that were <u>actually said</u>.

Speech marks — like an oral exam grade...

Speech marks always go in <u>pairs</u> — that's how you <u>tell them apart</u> from apostrophes. Make sure you <u>don't forget</u> to put <u>speech marks</u> round anything that a person or character has <u>actually said</u>.

SPEECH MARKS	# Two Rules for Speech Marks

Nearly there now — you'll need to remember <u>two big rules</u> when you're using <u>speech marks</u>.

The Speech Always Starts with a Capital Letter

"Let's have a game of pogo stick golf," said Claude.

<u>Here's</u> the capital letter.

Doug asked, "Where's the nineteenth hole?"

The speech bit <u>always</u> has a capital letter — even if it <u>isn't</u> at the start of the sentence.

It Ends with a Question Mark, Full Stop or Comma

"Who will fight me in a duel?" asked Louise.

 Who will fight me in a duel?

Here's the question mark.

Remember — spoken <u>questions</u> have to have a QUESTION MARK.

This speech <u>isn't</u> a question. It's got to end with a <u>full stop</u> instead.

Marco shouted, "I'm not afraid to fight."

"You're no match for me," replied Louise bravely.

This <u>isn't</u> a question either. The speech has <u>finished</u> but the sentence <u>hasn't</u> — you need a <u>comma</u> here.

Talk is cheap — if you're a budgie...

I know they look easy enough... but you'll <u>lose marks</u> if you forget these wee details. <u>Learn</u> these rules — <u>any</u> bit of speech must have a <u>capital</u> to start and a <u>full stop</u>, <u>comma</u> or <u>question mark</u> to end.

<u>Quoting</u>

<u>Quoting</u> is really important for your <u>essays</u> — especially any <u>literature essays</u> you've got to write. It means finding a bit from the <u>actual</u> poem, play or novel you're reading, and sticking it in your essay to <u>back up</u> a point you're making.

<u>Quoting</u> _is all about_ <u>Backing Up</u> _Your Points_

You're trying to <u>prove</u> a point — you've got to choose the <u>right bit</u> and then explain <u>why</u> it proves what you're saying.
Don't forget to use the <u>exact words</u> from the book, play or poem.

In the words of Cilla Black, "Surprise surprise."

How to <u>Quote</u> _from a_ <u>Novel</u> _or an_ <u>Article</u>

1) <u>This</u> is the bit you're <u>quoting</u>.

In _<u>Great Expectations</u>_, Wemmick's main concern is "portable property".

Portable property's my main concern too.

2) You've got to put <u>speech marks</u> around it.

3) Here's a <u>longer</u> bit of quoting. Remember the <u>speech marks</u>.

In Chapter XXI, Marlowe explains a little more about Patusan: "Patusan is a remote district of a native-ruled state, and the chief settlement bears the same name." (_<u>Lord Jim</u>_, p.161)

4) You must write <u>where</u> it came from.

<u>Never</u> quote <u>more</u> than <u>three lines</u>.
You <u>only</u> need the bit that <u>backs up</u> your point.

NO! This <u>doesn't</u> say <u>where</u> you're quoting from.

There is also a part where Dickens says that Wemmick has a postbox mouth.

WATCH OUT! <u>Don't</u> forget the <u>speech marks</u> or it gets seriously <u>confusing</u> to read.

<u>Quote tall tales — you'll have a high quota...</u>

Not the most fascinating stuff — but <u>quoting</u> is something you <u>don't</u> want to get wrong. It's all about using a bit from the book to <u>back up</u> your points. The <u>only way</u> to do that is by using the <u>exact words</u> in <u>speech marks</u>. And <u>never</u> make up anything you quote. That'll cost you lots of marks.

MORE ON QUOTATION	# Quoting from Poems and Plays

More about quoting, I'm afraid. <u>Poems</u> and <u>plays</u> cause <u>more problems</u> than novels.
The key is to make the bit you're <u>quoting</u> clearly <u>separate</u> from the <u>rest</u> of your essay.

How to <u>Quote</u> from a <u>Poem</u>

A garment for a city? I need a new tape-measure.

1) Here's a <u>phrase</u> from a poem — remember your speech marks.

The "beauty of the morning" is like a garment the City is wearing.

2) This time it's <u>four lines</u> of the poem.

3) Leave one line <u>blank</u> <u>before</u> and <u>after</u>.

Wordsworth describes Westminster at dawn.

This City now doth, like a garment, wear
The beauty of the morning; silent, bare,
Ships, towers, domes, theatres, and temples lie
Open unto the fields, and to the sky.
("Upon Westminster Bridge", lines 4-7)

4) Keep the <u>same words</u> at the <u>end</u> of each line as the original.

5) Keep the <u>same capitals</u>.

6) Give the <u>title</u>.

You've got to <u>copy</u> the lines <u>exactly</u>.
The <u>spelling</u> and <u>punctuation</u> must stay the <u>same</u>.

How to <u>Quote</u> from a <u>Play</u>

<u>Leave</u> a line <u>before</u> and <u>after</u> the quotation.

You need to give the <u>names</u> of the characters and the <u>stage directions</u>.

Juliet.	Saints do not move, though grant for prayers' sake.
Romeo.	Then move not while my prayer's effect I take.
	Thus from my lips, by thine, the sin is purg'd.
	[Kissing her.]

<u>Romeo and Juliet</u>, Act I, Scene V. lines 105-107.

Put where it <u>came from</u> too.

Quoting is like tracing — copy the lines exactly...

This looks like a really small thing but it can <u>still</u> make a difference to your <u>marks</u>. You've absolutely got to give the <u>exact words</u> from the original. And <u>never</u> give more than <u>four lines</u> from a poem or a play. The bit you quote is only <u>part</u> of your answer — you need to <u>explain</u> how it <u>backs up</u> your point.

Writing the Titles of Books

Here's another thing that you probably think is incredibly obvious — how to write the titles of plays, novels and poems. Unfortunately, loads of people seem to get it wrong.

You Must Underline the Titles of Novels and Plays

<u>Far from the Madding Crowd</u> is a novel by Thomas Hardy.

Don't use speech marks — just underline the title.

Shakespeare's play <u>A Midsummer Night's Dream</u>.

Did you like my Bottom?

Watch Out with Poems though...

1) Books or collections of poems get underlined too.

Ted Hughes' <u>Collected Poems</u>.

2) But be careful — you must use speech marks for the titles of individual poems.

3) This is one poem.

"The Whitsun Weddings" by Philip Larkin.
<u>The Whitsun Weddings</u> by Philip Larkin.

4) And this is a collection of poems.

Craig had an unusual way of collecting poems.

You need to underline the titles of poetry books or collections. But use speech marks with single poem titles.

You've Got to Copy the Title Exactly as it's Written

The <u>Wasteland</u> by TS Eliot.

= WRONG

'The' is part of the title too.

The <u>Waste Land</u> by TS Eliot.

Keep the capitals the same as the original.

Speech marks or underlining — a real title fight...

Titles are something you should never get wrong. All you need to do is make sure you copy the exact words and spellings, and keep the same capitals. Underline all titles except single poems.

Revision Summary

Punctuation can be a real hassle. That's why you need to go through every single one of these lovely questions. They're the only way to make completely sure that all of the important bits have sunk in. This is your chance to show what you've learned, so don't waste it by looking back over the section. Go through all the questions once first, then go back and look up the bits you couldn't remember. These questions are about helping you learn this stuff — in your exams they're much more serious than that. If you can sort this out now, then believe me, you won't have any problems with punctuation, and you won't be losing silly marks for carelessness.

1) When do you need to use capital letters?
2) Give an example of each case when you would need to use capitals.
3) What are exclamation marks used for?
4) Give two examples of sentences using exclamation marks.
5) What are the two things you should never do with exclamation marks?
6) What goes at the end of any sentence asking a question?
7) Write two example questions of your own.
8) Do the following sentences need question marks or not?   a) *Where can I find Pete.*
    b) *I was wondering where I could find Pete.* c) *How many people are coming tonight.*
9) What do you need commas for in lists?
10) Put commas and 'and' in the right places for this list; *"We met Dave Jeremy Pete Mike."*
11) What else do you need commas for?
12) Put a comma in the right place to show there are two clear points here:
    "We arrived at eight before they had finished clearing up."
13) Put commas in the following sentence to show which is the bit of extra information:
    "The Count hiding under a large black cape slipped into the bedchamber."
14) What's the difference between commas and dashes?
15) Give two examples of sentences using dashes.
16) When do you need to use apostrophes?
17) Put the apostrophes in the right places: a) *Ritas nose.* b) *Brians hand.* c) *Magnus face.*
18) Where do the apostrophes go for these plural forms?   a) *cats eyes.* b) *girls locker room.*
19) What is "we're" the short form of?
20) What is the short form of: a) *cannot?* b) *who is?* c) *I would?* d) *I have?*
21) What does it's mean?
22) What's the difference between it's and its?
23) Why is its like his?
24) What do speech marks show?
25) Put the speech marks into this sentence: *Give me the gun, said Mary.*
26) What's wrong with these sentences? Give the correct versions.
    a) *"Let's go shopping. said Andrew.* b) *Peter shouted I'll be back.*
27) What is quoting all about?
28) What's the biggest number of lines you should quote in one go?
29) How do you write the title of a book? Give one example. Then give the title of a single poem.
30) Learn these ten words and how to spell them. You need to get them absolutely perfect.

family	achieve	government	everything	changing
always	cousin	faithful	opinion	anxious

Sentences

Writing sentences isn't as tricky as you'd think. A sentence is just a <u>group of words</u> that <u>makes sense</u> on its own. Learn that and you're well on the way to picking up <u>loads of marks</u> for your writing.

Everything You Write Must Be in Sentences

Here's an ace tip — everything you write must be in <u>proper sentences</u>.
If it isn't in sentences, it won't be <u>clear</u>.
And you'll just be <u>throwing away marks</u>.

early ! bad
more bed

EEK! This <u>isn't</u> in proper sentences.

All Your Sentences Must Make Sense On Their Own

If you <u>can't understand</u> what it's supposed to mean, it <u>isn't</u> a proper sentence.

THE GOLDEN RULE:
Every sentence must make sense on its own.

There are two funny bits in the story.

You can see what this means even if you don't know exactly what it's about — it's a proper sentence.

I'm gone London, so they can.

This doesn't make sense — you can't tell what it means, so it isn't a proper sentence.

Each Sentence Needs to be Making a Clear Point

This fancy stuff about making sense sounds really grim.
All it means is <u>every sentence</u> you write has got to make a <u>clear point</u>.

I love carrot jam.

Sentences make sense — just ask a judge...

Sentences are funny things really — you use them <u>all the time</u>, so you don't think about them. But when it comes to <u>writing</u> them down, people make all sorts of <u>horrible mistakes</u>. Get it <u>clear</u> in your mind now — a sentence has to <u>make sense</u> on its own, and it has to make a <u>clear point</u> too.

How to Write a Sentence

There are two big rules you've got to learn about writing sentences. The good news is you really should know them already — just make sure you remember them EVERY SINGLE TIME.

① Sentences start with a capital letter.

② Sentences end with a full stop.

Learn these two simple rules.

Every Sentence Must Start with a Capital Letter

The frog was enormous.

Here's the capital.

Here's the capital.

Sean and Nick loved sailing.

Don't forget — names like Sean have a capital anyway.

Full Stops End Sentences

You need these little beggars to show that the sentence is totally finished.

A full stop ends the first sentence.

The dog ran into the wall. It staggered away looking dizzy.

Begin with a capital letter.

New sentence so you'll need a new capital letter.

Another full stop goes here.

Don't get this wrong — it's a capital offence...

Sentences really aren't that tricky to write — but remember every new sentence has to start with a capital letter and end with a full stop.   That's the big secret to writing sentences. Whatever you do, don't make daft mistakes like putting a comma instead of a full stop. You can wave goodbye to loads of easy marks if you make great big howlers like that. Get it learned.

Sentences and Verbs

This is the other big thing you need to know about sentences.
It's the hard bit too, I'm afraid. Every sentence has to have some kind of 'being' or 'doing' word.

Every Sentence Needs a 'Doing' or 'Being' Word

They bought a mad dog.

Here's the action in this sentence — it's the 'doing' word.

Jan was the world's first snail-tamer.

This is the 'being' word in the sentence.

Don't forget — the 'doing' or 'being' words in a sentence are called verbs.

Remember to stick a verb in every sentence you write.

You need a verb.

Make Sure the Verb is in the Right Form

When you're writing a verb in a sentence, say it out loud.
Think if it sounds right or not.

OUCH! This sounds wrong.

Jill like mouse sandwiches.

Jill likes mouse sandwiches.

Much better — that sounds right and it makes sense too.

NO!

The mice hates crusty bread.

Phew — that's better.

The mice hate crusty bread.

Verbs in sentences — where the action is...

This stuff about verbs is a real pain — it starts off alright, but gets tricky pretty fast. The really big thing to learn is never write a sentence without a verb. That's where you end up losing marks.

Revision Summary

A nice short section for you to learn here — but that doesn't mean you can get away without some more of those super revision questions. I know they're a pain, but they really can make a difference. Writing proper sentences will seriously improve any essay work you do. The examiners will be able to see exactly what you're saying. Your work will be clear — and that's the biggest problem most people have. Give yourself a better chance — work through these questions and see how much you know. Go on, surprise yourself.

1) What is a sentence?
2) Why do you need to write in sentences?
3) Is this a proper sentence? If it isn't, then write a proper sentence instead: *The cold night air.*
4) Is this a sentence? Write a proper sentence instead if it isn't: *It was a cold, dark night.*
5) Is this a sentence? Write a proper sentence instead if it isn't: *Leanne likes to scream loudly.*
6) Is this a sentence? Write a proper sentence instead if it isn't: *Cassius about Caesar.*
7) What's the rule about capital letters and full stops in sentences?
8) What's wrong with this sentence? *She found Mr Darcy strangely attractive,*
9) What's the rule about sentences and verbs?
Put these verbs into the right form in each sentence. They're in the wrong form at the moment:
10) *Andy eat fish and chips every day.*
11) *My friends likes going clubbing.*
12) *I would likes to get to know you better.*
13) *Susanna always want to go shopping.*
14) *Harry kick every cat he see.*
    (There are two verbs in this sentence. Make sure you put both into the right form)
15) Learn these ten tricky words, and don't forget to make sure you can spell them perfectly too:

beginning	attitude	seize	rhyme	servant
disappeared	fought	eerie	conscience	emphasise

Adjectives

Adjectives always sound a bit posh to me. They aren't really — they're just describing words. You use them to say what things are like — like 'big', 'famous' or 'yellow'.

Adjectives Describe Things and People

1) *I knew that the deadly vampire bats were coming.*

Put in a scary adjective to tell them more about the vampire bats.

I knew that the vampire bats were coming.

You've only got the bare facts here — nothing else.

2) *Sindy wants to meet a tall, blond and handsome man.*

Three gorgeous adjectives describing the person Sindy wants to meet. They make her sound quite choosy.

1 out of 3's not bad...

Sindy wants to meet a man.

If you leave out the adjectives, she sounds a bit desperate.

You must use adjectives in your writing — they make it clearer.

Use Adjectives to Make Your Sentences More Interesting

A dark, mysterious figure appeared in the doorway.

These spooky adjectives grab your attention. It wouldn't be as creepy without them.

'Ey up!

Invisible ink — it makes your writing clear...

Writing interesting sentences is the big secret to getting the marks you need in your exam. That means you really need to know what an adjective does — scribble it down somewhere and learn it.

USING ADJECTIVES | # Making Things Clearer

There's one big thing you've got to keep in mind with adjectives.
Every adjective you write must tell you more about the noun it goes with.

Adjectives Tell You More About the Noun

They're a fantastic way to give a clearer picture of what you're talking about.

1) Sizes

> Harry the monster was tall and broad.

2) Colours

> His new coat was red and black.

> I'll shoot the wax outta your ears at 20 paces.

Eagle-Eye Jane

3) Shapes

> Her eyes were round like dinner plates.

4) Feelings

These vicious adjectives describe how prison makes you feel.

> Prison is a horrible, cruel place.

> Alan was charming and sweet.

Two cute adjectives to show how Alan makes you feel.

Careful though — your adjectives must make sense together.

He wore a scruffy, smart suit = DOESN'T MAKE SENSE

Describing sizes — the long and short of it...

Adjectives are pretty friendly words really. You've got to use them to write clearer sentences.
Make sure you learn the four things adjectives tell you right now. It'll help your writing in the long run.

Describing Actions

It's a tricky business, all this describing — but your writing will pick up some <u>big marks</u> if you can get this stuff <u>clear</u> in your head.

Adverbs Describe How an Action is Done

1) *He played <u>well</u> in the first half.*

Here's the adverb telling you <u>how</u> he played.

He played in the first half.

This only tells you <u>what</u> happened — it hasn't got any emotion to it.

2) *<u>Slowly</u> and <u>carefully</u>, the shark swam towards Rufus.*

Here there are <u>two dramatic adverbs</u> telling you <u>how</u> the shark was swimming.

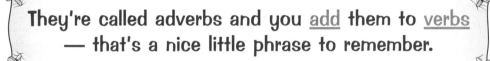

They're called adverbs and you <u>add</u> them to <u>verbs</u> — that's a nice little phrase to remember.

You Must Use Adverbs to Get Better Marks

Adverbs are great for making sentences <u>come to life</u>, especially in stories.

Zorrina leapt up <u>quickly</u>, waving her sword <u>bravely</u>.

These words make the sentence <u>more exciting</u>.

Add verbs — for better tasting sentences...

Adverbs are strange wee words — you use them <u>all the time</u> when you're talking, but you just don't think about it. That's why you need to learn <u>how to use them</u> when you write. They're a brilliant way to make stories <u>exciting</u> and <u>fun</u> to read — after all, they <u>describe</u> the <u>how</u>, not just the what.

USING ADVERBS WITH ADJECTIVES

Adverbs and Adjectives Together

Adverbs are smashing really — you can use them in all sorts of ways.
Apart from adverbs with verbs, the main one you <u>need to know</u> about is adverbs with <u>adjectives</u>.

Adverbs with Adjectives Tell You How

1)   Sally looked <u>totally</u> different when she dyed her hair black.

> This little adverb tells you <u>how different</u> she looked
> — remember, <u>different</u> is an <u>adjective</u>.

I just felt like a change.

2)   Laura's stories are <u>very</u> funny.

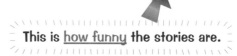

> This is <u>how funny</u> the stories are.

3)   Ed is <u>quite</u> friendly to everyone.

> This tells you <u>how friendly</u> Ed is — just 'quite'.

Morning everybody.

4)   He is <u>completely</u> crazy.

> Tells you <u>how crazy</u> he is.

5)   We arrived <u>just</u> <u>too</u> late.

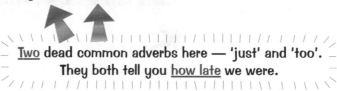

> <u>Two</u> dead common adverbs here — 'just' and 'too'.
> They both tell you <u>how late</u> we were.

The words of commercials — ad verbs...

It really isn't as difficult as it looks — just remember that adverbs tell you <u>how</u> in a sentence.
And don't forget — you can use them with <u>adjectives</u> as well as <u>verbs</u>. They're a big <u>mark winner</u>.

Images

Images always sound like something out of a film — but you can put images in your writing too.
They're a way of giving the reader a picture of what something is like just by using words.
Pretty clever really — they're something you should definitely be using in your writing.

Saying One Thing is Like Something Else

Here's the image.

1) Max's shadow was terrifying <u>like a huge monster</u>.

2) The lights of the city shone <u>like stars in the night sky</u>.

This is an image of what the lights <u>look like</u>.

Images tell you what the thing is <u>like</u>,
<u>not</u> what it actually is.

3) The pig danced <u>like</u> a ballerina,

but she sang <u>like</u> a toad.

You Can Also Use 'As' in Image Sentences

I wish I were as fast as a cheetah...

They ate <u>as if they hadn't eaten for years</u>.

This isn't actually true, but it helps you <u>imagine</u> how hungry they were.

He was <u>as fast as a cheetah</u>.

Shakespeare's image — just 'as you like it'...

Images are pretty cool — and all you need to <u>make</u> them is one of those helpful words '<u>as</u>' or '<u>like</u>'.
But be careful — <u>don't</u> put <u>too many</u> images in your written work, just a <u>few</u> to brighten things up.

| COMPARATIVES | ## Comparing Things |

This is another sort of sentence that grabs the reader's mind and joggles it awake.
Instead of just writing a boring old fact, you say that one thing is better or worse than another.

There are Two Top Ways to Compare Things

(1) For short words like 'tall', 'short', 'happy' and 'low', just take the adjective...

...and stick on '-er + than'.

Here the 'y' in happy changes to 'i'.

Martin is taller than Natalie.

tall + er + than

Why is he happier than Sheila?

(2) For longer words and all other comparisons...

Angie is more beautiful than Jane.

= if the first thing's better than the second one.

Angie is less cheerful than Jane.

= if the first thing isn't as good as the second one.

Angie   Jane

Angie is as tall as Jane.

= if two things are the same, you need to use 'as...as'.

Shall I compare thee to a summer's day — nah...

This stuff is really worth learning. It's the sort of thing examiners give plenty of extra marks for.
Watch out for one big mistake though — you've absolutely got to remember to put in the 'than' and
the second thing you're comparing. Without them you won't even be writing proper sentences.

Best and Worst

Sometimes comparing two things <u>isn't enough</u> — you need to say who or what is the <u>best</u> or <u>worst</u>. Make sure you get <u>all</u> of this stuff <u>learned</u> — some of it can be pretty tough.

Learn these Common Forms for Best and Worst

Learn these dead <u>common forms</u>. You'll need them handy if you want to get good marks.

good	better	best
bad	worse	worst
much/many	more	most
little	less	least
few	fewer	fewest

Leo could do the <u>best</u> two-footed karate kicks in the country.

Add -est to the End of Short Adjectives

He had the long<u>est</u> stick and the heavi<u>est</u> rucksack.

Longest means the <u>most long</u>.

Heaviest means the <u>most heavy</u>. The 'y' in 'heavy' <u>changes</u> to '<u>i</u>'.

They were the ugli<u>est</u> insects I have ever seen.

This word tells you just <u>how ugly</u> the bugs were.

Don't forget — 'long', 'heavy' and 'ugly' are all <u>adjectives</u>.

It was the best of pages, it was the worst...

Adding <u>-est</u> is an easy way to talk about the best or worst — but remember you can <u>only</u> do it with <u>short forms</u>. And <u>don't</u> ever try to use 'than' with an 'est' form — it's wrong, and you'll <u>lose</u> yourself loads of hard-earned marks. Make sure you <u>learn</u> the table of <u>common forms</u> right away.

Most and Least

This is where it gets a bit clever — for <u>longer words</u>, it doesn't sound right if you add '-est'. Instead you'll need to bring in that smashing little word '<u>most</u>'.

You Must Use 'Most' with Long Adjectives

Here's the <u>adjective</u>.

1) He was the <u>most</u> amazing dancer at the party.

You just add '<u>most</u>'.
There's no such word as 'amazingest'.

Same here — you've got to have '<u>most</u>' with the adjective '<u>beautiful</u>'.

2) She was the <u>most</u> beautiful woman Boris knew.

Never Use 'Most' and '-est' Together

With 'smelly' you <u>can</u> use '-est'.
<u>Don't</u> use 'most' as well.

Stefan was the <u>smelliest</u> Spice Boy,

but he was the <u>most</u> interesting one to talk to.

You've got to use <u>most</u> here —
'interestingest' sounds stupid.

The Opposite of 'Most' is 'Least'

One more own goal
and I'll have
beaten the record.

This time you're adding '<u>least</u>'.
Don't put 'less' by mistake.

This is the <u>adjective</u> here. You can use
'<u>least</u>' with short <u>or</u> long adjectives.

United are the <u>least</u> popular team in England.

Go on — get the most out of this page...

'<u>Most</u>' and 'least' are cool words — they make your sentences dead <u>clear</u>. The best thing about them is you <u>don't</u> have to change the <u>adjective</u> at all. And <u>don't</u> use 'most' and '-est' together.

SECTION FIVE — WRITING BETTER SENTENCES

Don't Use 'And' All the Time

'And' is a weird little word that shows up <u>all over</u> the place.
It's a kind of gluey word — you use it to <u>stick</u> short sentences together and make a <u>longer one</u>.
But that's where the problem starts — <u>too many</u> 'ands' mean your writing gets incredibly <u>boring</u>.

Don't Use 'And' or 'And Then' All the Time

MEGA BORING

John went to the bank <u>and</u> he went to the shop <u>and</u> he bought some socks <u>and</u> he didn't buy any pants, <u>and then</u> he went home.

You <u>can't tell</u> which is the <u>most important bit</u> of this sentence.

Too Many 'Ands' Can Send You DOWN ONE GRADE

This is <u>awful</u>. It <u>isn't</u> clear to follow. If you write like this for your GCSE, the examiners'll think you <u>don't know</u> anything about sentences — which could take you <u>down</u> one whole grade.

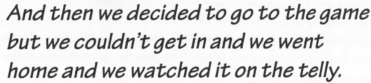

And then we decided to go to the game but we couldn't get in and we went home and we watched it on the telly.

Then we decided to go to the game, but we couldn't get in. We went home instead and watched it on the telly.

Splitting this into <u>two sentences</u> makes it much <u>clearer</u>.

Don't be an octopus — with too many 'ands...

Phew — this is a <u>really important bit</u>, I'm afraid. <u>Don't</u> use 'and' or 'and then' too much in your writing. The examiners will think you <u>can't</u> write clear sentences if you do it a lot — and you could drop down <u>one whole grade</u>. It's much <u>better</u> to write <u>short, clear sentences</u> than long, boring ones.

Keeping Long Sentences Clear

Long sentences always look pretty smart, but they can end up being really confusing too.
You'll find yourself losing marks for writing them — unless you learn how to keep them clear.

Don't Let Your Sentences Go On for Too Long

> The monster crashed through the city, looking for Ellen and eventually found her in the park, where she was sitting underneath a tree, where she'd been all day.

ZZZzz! There's too much stuff for one sentence. It's confusing and boring to read.

Every Sentence You Write Should Make Clear Points

> The monster crashed through the city, looking for Ellen.

Much clearer now — you can see exactly what the two points of this sentence are.

Always check the main point is clear in every sentence you write.

> It found her in the park, sitting under a tree.

This sentence makes two points but it's still clear.

I'll give you a clear point mate!

> She had been there all day.

Just the one point here.

Sentences are like swords — get the point...

This is quite a tricky thing to get right — the bad news is there isn't a rule that says when a sentence is too long. You've just got to be really careful — make sure each sentence is dead clear.

Sentences with 'No' or 'Not'

'No' and 'not' are those great little words for saying you <u>don't like</u> things, or <u>don't want</u> to do them. Unfortunately, sentences with <u>negatives</u> like these are really easy to get <u>wrong</u>.

Never Use Don't and No in the Same Sentence

I don't like them much.

This is **WRONG:**

I don't like nobody here.

We don't like you either!

I <u>like</u> <u>no</u>body here.

Here's <u>one</u> correct way to say it...

I <u>don't</u> like <u>any</u>body here.

...and here's <u>another</u> — just don't confuse them.

<u>Don't</u> stick '<u>no</u>' in sentences with '<u>-n't</u>' or '<u>not</u>'. You've got to use '<u>any</u>' instead.

We haven't got no milk. = **WRONG**

 Phew — that's better. ➤ *We <u>haven't</u> got <u>any</u> milk.*

'Ain't' Isn't a Word — Use 'Hasn't', 'Haven't' or 'Isn't'

 NO!

I ain't got none. ➤

This is right.

I <u>haven't</u> got <u>any</u>.

'<u>None</u>' is like '<u>no</u>' — if you use '<u>-n't</u>' you've got to use '<u>any</u>'.

But I haven't got any hair tonic!

Take good photos — don't waste negatives...

These three examples may not look all that important — but mistakes like these will <u>cost you</u> lots of <u>silly marks</u>. Just make sure you learn the <u>correct sentences</u> on this page. <u>Scribble</u> them on a bit of paper, cover them up and <u>learn them</u>. It'll be worth it — you really <u>don't</u> want to lose these marks.

| USING VARIED VOCABULARY | **_Using Different Words_** |

This might sound a bit strange — but it's true.
You'll pick up lots of extra marks if you use lots of different and new ways to say the same thing.

Try using Different Words for 'Said'

1) "I hate Mondays!" Elizabeth wailed.

This tells you how miserable Elizabeth was feeling.

2) "We are not amused," muttered the Queen.

Here 'muttered' means the Queen was speaking quietly.

3) "That's the best cup of tea I've ever had," declared Eric.

This is a really bold word — Eric's saying exactly what he thinks.

Don't just write 'said' all the time — it's really boring.
Stick in a few of these words instead.

whispered	shouted	gasped	asked	replied
cried	yelled	repeated	commented	sobbed
complained	remarked	screamed	demanded	exclaimed

My favourite colour shouts at you — yeller...

'Said' is one of those lazy old words you don't think about. You keep putting it in, and pretty soon your answer is dead boring to read. The only way to avoid that is by using different words. Start by learning the table of words at the bottom of the page — they'll definitely help you liven things up.

Using Interesting Words

<u>Interesting words</u> are a top way to kick your work back to life when you write.
Don't forget to <u>learn</u> this stuff carefully — it could make a <u>big difference</u> to your <u>final mark</u>.

Don't *Write the Same Words* Over *and* Over

Everybody <u>knows</u> it's a play.
You <u>don't need</u> to tell them twice.

<u>Don't</u> repeat the names in the <u>same sentence</u>.

In the play <u>Romeo and Juliet</u>, Romeo and Juliet fall in love. The play has lots of beautiful poetry about Romeo and Juliet's love.

'Beautiful' doesn't mean <u>anything</u> unless you say <u>why</u> it was beautiful.

This is the <u>third time</u> you've written their names in two sentences — now that's <u>seriously dull</u>.

This is <u>much better</u> — it <u>doesn't</u> repeat words and it sounds really <u>enthusiastic</u>.

You're useless! I said "poetry," not "pottery"

In <u>Romeo and Juliet</u>, the two main characters fall passionately in love. The play is full of beautiful rhyming poetry which expresses their longing and their confusion.

The last sentence explains <u>why</u> the poetry is beautiful.

Watch Out *for Words like 'Nice' and 'Beautiful'*

Words like 'nice', 'exciting', 'beautiful' and 'excellent' can get <u>extremely boring</u>.
You need to find more <u>interesting</u> words to say the same things.

Charming	*Thrilling*	*Gorgeous*	*Brilliant*
Perfect	*Dramatic*	*Elegant*	*Superb*
Magnificent	*Sensational*	*Stunning*	*Incredible*
Delightful	*Electrifying*	*Graceful*	*Wonderful*

Boring words — like 'drill', 'woodpecker' etc...

This may sound silly — but <u>boring sentences</u> are a real turn off. You'll just be <u>wasting</u> easy marks.
All you need to do is spend some time <u>learning</u> words to use when you write. In fact, you should
start with the <u>box</u> on this page. It's very simple — learn <u>more words</u> and you'll get <u>better marks</u>.

62

Revision Summary

Another section done... You've guessed it — time for some more of those cracking revision questions. I know this is the boring bit, but believe me, it's worth it. You've got to make sure you know absolutely all the stuff in this section before moving on. The only way you can guarantee yourself decent marks is by writing interesting and clear sentences. That means working your way through all these little beggars. If you get stuck at all, then you'll have to go back over those pages again. It isn't much fun, I'm afraid — just grit your teeth and get on with it.

1) What are adjectives used for?
2) Add adjectives to these three sentences to make them a bit more interesting:
   a) *Tess was afraid of Alec.*   b) *He could hear the guns.*   c) *Romeo likes girls.*
3) Write a sentence using adjectives to describe the colour and size of something.
4) Write a sentence using at least two adjectives to describe how you feel about school.
5) What do adverbs do, and why should you use them?
6) Add adverbs to these sentences to liven them up: a) *Estella hurt Pip.*   b) *He arrived late.*
7) What does an image do?
8) Write a sentence which contains an image.
9) What do you add to verbs like 'short', 'happy' and 'low' to compare things?
10) When do you use 'more...than'? Give an example sentence.
11) When do you use 'less...than'? Give an example sentence.
12) When do you use 'as...as'? Give an example sentence.
13) Give three sentences about the best or the worst.
14) Write one sentence using 'most' with a long adjective, and another one using 'least'.
15) Why shouldn't you use 'and' all the time?
16) Rewrite this sentence as two shorter sentences: *They were surrounded by the enemy forces and they were running out of ammunition and then they decided to surrender.*
17) What is the secret of writing clear sentences?
18) Rewrite this sentence as shorter sentences, making only one or two clear points:
    The rebels decided to escape under cover of darkness but the enemy were ready for them and as every rebel soldier made a run for it, he was captured and taken away to prison where he would be made to confess to his crimes.
19) What's wrong with this sentence?   *I don't want nobody fighting.*
20) Give the two correct ways you could write the sentence in question 19).
21) Give the correct version of this sentence: *I ain't got none.*
22) Think of a different word for 'said' here: *"Don't leave me!" said Ethel the Pirate's daughter.*
23) Think of a different word for 'said' here: *"Look out!" said Peter.*
24) Think of another word for 'said' here: *"Help!" said Captain Rodney.*
25) Why shouldn't you write the same words over and over?
26) Rewrite this with a different word for 'nice':   *Kate thought boxing was nice.*
27) Rewrite this with a different word for 'beautiful':   *The words of the song were beautiful.*
28) Rewrite this with another word for 'excellent':   *He was an excellent swordsman.*
29) Rewrite this with another word for 'exciting':   *Pete found bullfighting very exciting.*
30) Learn these ten useful words, and make sure you can spell them too.

rhythm	guess	formally	extremely	foreign
immature	weird	separate	compare	business

SECTION FIVE — WRITING BETTER SENTENCES

Paragraphs Make Things Clear

Paragraphs are <u>horrible things</u> — you know you <u>ought</u> to use them, but they're a big hassle.
I know they're a <u>pain</u> to remember, but it's <u>really important</u> you know how they <u>help</u> your work.

> A paragraph is a group of sentences. These sentences talk about the same thing, or follow on from each other.

Paragraphs *Make Your Writing Clearer*

All of the <u>sentences</u> in a paragraph are <u>related</u> to each other.
Every time you start a <u>new paragraph</u>, you're showing that <u>something new</u> has happened.

> ...in the light of the full moon.
>   The whole camp was quiet as Brutus sat alone in his tent. He couldn't sleep, nor could he stop thinking about Portia. Why did she have to die?
>   Then he heard something — something strange, like a distant whispering sound...

The <u>ideas</u> in this paragraph are all related.
They're about Brutus sitting in his tent.
When something <u>new</u> happens, you start a <u>new</u> paragraph.

Have a stab at learning this... I did.

WATCH OUT! <u>Everything</u> you write <u>must</u> be in <u>paragraphs</u> — or it could <u>cost</u> you big time. You could <u>drop</u> a <u>whole grade</u> if you forget them.

Portia — thought that was a type of car...

Paragraphs <u>aren't</u> as pointless as you might think. Unless you write in paragraphs, it'll be impossible for anyone to <u>understand</u> what your writing is all about. And that means you <u>won't</u> get as many <u>marks</u>. There's only one thing for it — make sure you <u>know</u> what a paragraph is and how to <u>use</u> it.

64

Starting a New Paragraph

<u>When</u> to finish one paragraph and start a new one is a <u>tricky</u> business. It isn't always obvious — you'll just have to <u>learn the rules</u> and use your head. Start with the golden rule right now.

This is the <u>Golden Rule</u> for Paragraphs — <u>Learn</u> <u>it</u>

Start a <u>new paragraph</u> every time something <u>changes</u>.

1) <u>When You Talk about a New Person</u>

This paragraph is about Liam.

Time for a new paragraph — there's a <u>new person</u>.

Nuts!

> Liam sat on the side of the stage. He couldn't believe it. His guitar was broken, and without it he wouldn't be able to play at the school concert. He felt like crying.
> Then he saw Keith. Keith was a skinny, ill-looking boy who always got picked on. He was carrying an enormous guitar case.

2) <u>Each Time a Person Speaks</u>

Someone <u>new</u> is speaking so you need to <u>change</u> paragraph.

> "I'll find him," muttered Donald. "He won't get away this time.
> "What makes you so sure?" asked Mickey.
> "What's going on guys?" A figure stepped out of the darkness. It was Elvis.

Just think King Midas — he had a golden rule...

This stuff is dead easy to learn — just remember that <u>every time</u> you write about a <u>new person</u> you need a <u>new paragraph</u>. Simple really — so get it <u>learned</u>. And don't forget you need a <u>new paragraph</u> whenever a person <u>speaks</u> in your writing. <u>Learn</u> this and you're well on the way.

New Places or Times

Here are the other <u>big reasons</u> for starting a <u>new paragraph</u> — make sure you <u>learn</u> them right now. And remember to <u>use</u> them when you're writing — they'll seriously <u>boost</u> your <u>marks</u>.

3) <u>When You Start Writing about a New Place</u>

This paragraph is about the <u>playing fields</u>.

> The playing fields were quiet and peaceful. There was no one around except Pete. He listened to the song of the distant birds and sighed happily.
> Further down the valley, near Chorlbury, a huge cloud of dust rose into the summer sky, as the rebel elephant army raced towards the school. They were coming to free the students.

Here's a <u>new paragraph</u>, because this is happening <u>somewhere else</u>.

Don't forget — you <u>change</u> paragraph to show you're writing about something <u>new</u> or something <u>different</u>.

4) <u>When Your Answer Moves to a Different Time</u>

The first paragraph's about <u>five o'clock</u>.

> By five o'clock, Edwin was angry. Shirley was late again, and the flower he'd bought was starting to droop.
> Six o'clock came, and still she didn't appear. Enough was enough. Stuffing his flower into a rubbish bin, Edwin went home.
> Three years before, Edwin had been stood up. He had never seen or heard from the girl again, and he didn't fancy going through another emotional crisis.

This one's gone <u>forward</u> to a <u>different time</u>.

Here's one about the <u>past</u>.

<u>Changing paragraphs — any time, any place...</u>

You've got to use a <u>new paragraph</u> every time you <u>change</u> time or place. That's the bottom line. And <u>don't worry</u> about how <u>long</u> or <u>short</u> your paragraphs are — just make sure they're totally <u>clear</u>.

HOW TO START & END PARAGRAPHS

How to Write a Paragraph

The <u>biggest problem</u> you'll have with paragraphs is working out <u>how</u> to make them <u>clear</u>.
You need to make it <u>mind-bogglingly obvious</u> to the examiner where your paragraphs <u>start</u> and <u>end</u>.
If you don't, it'll look like you <u>haven't</u> written paragraphs at all — bringing your marks right <u>down</u>.

You've Got to Leave a Space on the First Line

Here's a <u>brand new</u> paragraph — so you need to leave a <u>space</u>.

Don't forget — a new paragraph means a <u>new space</u>.

Space?

This is a very important rule. Every new paragraph must have a space between the margin and the first word.

Leave another space every time you start a new paragraph. This shows you're writing about something different. It'll also make your work look much neater — which means more marks.

Always remember the <u>gaps</u> at the <u>start</u> and <u>end</u> of every paragraph.

Leave a Gap at the End of the Last Sentence

Here's how to end your paragraphs. Just finish the last sentence and leave the rest of that line blank — even if there's a lot of line left.

Then start your new paragraphs with the proper space — that's the way to do it.

Just leave the <u>rest</u> of this line <u>blank</u>.

I can't wait till the end of my sentence.

And remember the <u>space</u> for the <u>next paragraph</u>.

Be an astronaut — learn to love space...

This stuff is the key to making your work <u>easy to read</u>. It's <u>not enough</u> to hand in any old mess — you need to make <u>absolutely sure</u> the examiner can see where your paragraphs <u>start</u> and <u>end</u>. They'll <u>definitely</u> have to give you the <u>marks</u> then. Remember — it's all about <u>space</u>.

Revision Summary

Paragraphs can be slippery customers. The trick is knowing when to finish one paragraph and start the next. Just remember that as long as you make your paragraphs really clear, with plenty of space, then your written work will start to look much easier to read. These questions are here to help you go over what you've learned in this section. If you can't do all of them, then don't worry. Go back over the bits you aren't sure about and have another try. This is all about testing yourself. It's the only way to be totally sure that you've learned it.

1) What is a paragraph?
2) Why do you need to write in paragraphs?
3) What is the golden rule for paragraphs?
4) What's the rule for paragraphs and people?
5) What's the rule for paragraphs and speech?
6) What's the rule for paragraphs and places?
7) What's the rule for paragraphs and time changes?
8) What do you need to do on the first line of every paragraph?
9) What do you have to do at the end of the last sentence of a paragraph?
10) Put the following passage into proper paragraphs:

   At the fourth chime, Ellen pushed the door open slowly, so it wouldn't make a noise. She tiptoed down the stairs carefully, just in case there was a creaky step. "What are you doing?" said her uncle, stepping from the shadows of the grandfather clock. "Nothing!" gasped Ellen in shock. "It doesn't look like nothing," replied her uncle, in a sinister voice.

11) Write three paragraphs about the last book you read, making sure you follow all the rules.
12) Write three paragraphs of a story, using the rules in this section.
13) Write three paragraphs about where you live, remembering the rule about places.
14) Write a short essay about the last three years of your life. Don't forget the rule about paragraphs and time changes.
15) Learn these ten tremendous words off by heart — and how to spell them.

spiteful	autumn	succeed	humorous	theatre
likeable	argue	arguing	enemies	weight

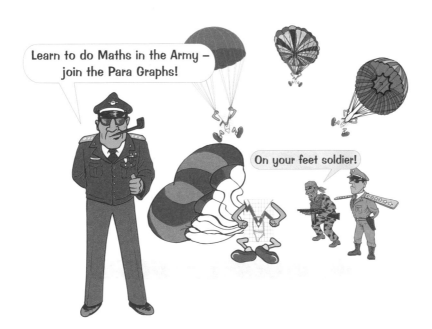

Learn to do Maths in the Army — join the Para Graphs!

On your feet soldier!

PRACTISE/PRACTICE & PAST/PASSED

Practise/Practice & Past/Passed

This is about those words you love to <u>hate</u> — the ones that <u>sound</u> the same but <u>mean</u> different things. There's no way around these tricky devils <u>except</u> to scribble them down and <u>learn</u> them.

Practise _is a Verb but_ Practice _is a Noun_

'Practise' is a <u>doing word</u> — a verb.
For <u>verbs</u> you use an 's'.

I _practise_ my serve.

I love tennis _practice_.

Tennis practice is a <u>noun</u> — a thing you go to.
For <u>nouns</u> you use a 'c'.

It's the Same as Advise & Advice, or Devise & Device

With these ones it's easier to remember, because they <u>sound</u> different.

I asked Tom to _advise_ me.

Tom's _advice_ was useless.

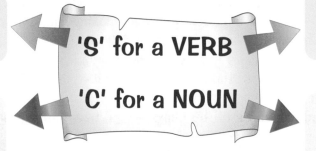
'S' for a VERB

'C' for a NOUN

Shelly had _devised_ a new evil scheme.

She was building an enormous _device_.

Don't confuse Passed with Past

Passed with -ed is an <u>action</u>, but past with -t <u>is not</u>.

She ran on, _past_ the church.

She'd known him in the _past_.

I _passed_ the ball to Kate.

Kate _passed_ through the hole.

Blunt knives and railways — pointless training...

'Practise' and 'practice' <u>always</u> cause trouble. They're two of the <u>hardest</u> words to get right in the whole English language. Remember, '<u>practice</u>' is a <u>thing</u>, an <u>event</u> or an <u>idea</u>. '<u>Practise</u>' is a <u>verb</u>.

Affect/Effect & Accept/Except

Here are two sneaky pairs of words that can really <u>annoy</u> you — unless you <u>learn</u> them carefully.

Affect *is the Action but* Effect *is the Result*

Andy's balloon didn't <u>affect</u> me.

<u>Affect</u> is an <u>action</u>
which is influencing something.

<u>Effect</u> is the <u>result</u>
of an action.

Andy's fan had a nasty *effect*.

Accept *is Totally Different from* Except

1) Accept is a <u>verb</u>. It means '<u>agreeing to</u>' something, or '<u>receiving</u>' something.

Bill wanted her to <u>accept</u> *a Valentine's present.*

2) This means he <u>couldn't agree</u> to it.

Her angry reaction was <u>unacceptable</u>.

3) Except means '<u>not including</u>'.

Everyone received flowers <u>except</u> *her.*

She didn't like being the only <u>exception</u>.

Wimbledon weather — the trickle down effect...

More learning, I'm afraid, but it's the <u>only way</u> to make sure you <u>don't</u> muddle these words.
Learn this — '<u>accept</u>' and '<u>affect</u>' are <u>verbs</u>, '<u>except</u>' means <u>not including</u> and '<u>effect</u>' is a <u>result</u>.

| WHERE/WEAR/WERE THERE/THEIR/THEY'RE | # Words like 'Where' and 'There' |

It's about to get even <u>harder</u>... Some common mistakes are made with groups of <u>three words</u> that all <u>sound</u> the <u>same</u>. Talk about a major headache — you'll need to learn <u>all of them</u>.

Where, Were and Wear

① **WHERE** is used for <u>places</u> and <u>positions</u>.

Where is my hat?

② **WEAR** is what you do with clothes, shoes and jewellery — you <u>wear</u> them.

You're <u>wearing</u> it!

③ **WERE** is the past form of <u>are</u>.

They <u>were</u> not great friends.

> If you're not sure about 'were' in a sentence, stick 'are' in instead. If it still makes sense then <u>were</u> is definitely right.

There, Their and They're

① **THERE** goes with <u>where</u> — it's about places and positions.

Frank and Fran are over <u>there</u>.

② **THEIR** means <u>it belongs to them</u>.

They told me it's <u>their</u> money.

③ **THEY'RE** is short for "<u>they are</u>".
Look at the page on <u>apostrophes</u> (see P.37).

I reckon <u>they're</u> thieving scoundrels.

My coat's always tired — I keep wearing it out...

'There' and 'where' are about <u>places</u> and <u>positions</u>; 'their' means <u>belonging to them</u>; 'they're' is <u>short</u> for '<u>they are</u>'; 'wear' is about <u>clothes</u>, and 'were' is the <u>past</u> of '<u>are</u>'. That's your lot — <u>learn</u> it.

To/Too/Two and Off/Of

I hate these little words. They're much too easy to get wrong, especially if you're in a rush. The thing is, lots of mistakes like these make the Examiners think your work is poor.

To/Too/Two — They're All Different

1. **TO** means towards or is part of a verb.

She likes to ride. = Part of a verb.

She's going to Mars. = Towards.

2. **TWO** is just the number '2'.

Two million pounds. Think of tw for 'twice'.

3. **TOO** means "too much" or "also".

His neck's too long... = Too much.

...and he's hairy too. = Also.

'Off' Means 'Away From', the Rest of the Time Use 'Of'

OFF is like "away from".

OF is just a linking word.

JANUARY SALE
Special Offer
Christmas Trees
35% off

This means 35% taken away from the price.

Your head's full of rubbish.

Of links the words together.

A packet of crisps.

Never Ever Write 'Off Of'

These are both OK.

He jumped off of the bridge.

NO!

He jumped off the bridge.

He jumped from the bridge.

This cheese is off — it's on its way to Brazil...

Time to scribble each group of words down in rough, and learn them carefully. There's no other way.

| THEM & THOSE | **Them or Those** |

Here's a <u>mistake</u> that can often come about in your writing because of the way you <u>speak</u>.
A lot of people try to <u>write</u> things like "I like them books."   Unfortunately, that's completely <u>wrong</u>.

Don't <u>Use</u> 'Them' When You Mean 'Those'

This is **WRONG** ➡️ *I hate <u>them aliens</u>.*

1) You <u>can't</u> use '<u>them</u>' and '<u>aliens</u>' together. You've got to use '<u>those</u>' instead.

I hate <u>those</u> aliens.

2) '<u>Those</u>' is used for pointing <u>specific</u> things out, like the aliens.

3) '<u>Them</u>' is a form of the pronoun '<u>they</u>', so you <u>can't</u> use it with other words.

I hate <u>them</u>.

4) Remember — 'them' is a <u>pronoun</u> — you put it in <u>instead</u> of the noun 'aliens'.

'<u>Them</u>' goes <u>on its own</u>.
<u>Never</u> put it with a noun.

NO! ➡️ *<u>Them</u> weights are heavy.*

This is right. ➡️ *<u>Those</u> weights are heavy.*

Those two words — don't you just hate them...

<u>Don't</u> write anything like "Pass me them chips", or "Them books aren't yours." Sentences like that are <u>wrong</u>, and they really <u>won't</u> help to impress the Examiner. '<u>Them</u>' is a form of '<u>they</u>' — get that clear. You can <u>only</u> use it <u>instead</u> of a noun. '<u>Those</u>' is used <u>with</u> a noun for <u>pointing</u> things out.

Lend/Borrow, Teach/Learn, Principle

Three pairs that you really <u>shouldn't</u> confuse — they mean <u>different</u> things, so get learning.

Lend *Something TO Someone, Borrow It FROM Them*

Can I lend your notes? ← **NO!** Not right. <u>Lend</u> means to <u>give</u> something out.

Can I <u>borrow</u> your notes?

No way!

I'm <u>taking</u> your notes, so I'm <u>borrowing from</u> you.

OUCH! Not right. <u>Borrow</u> means to <u>take</u> something.

Can you borrow me your notes?

You're <u>giving</u> the notes, so you're <u>lending to</u> me.

Can you <u>lend</u> me your notes?

Teach *and* Learn *are Opposites*

I teach.

<u>Teaching</u> is <u>giving out</u> knowledge.
<u>Learning</u> is <u>taking</u> knowledge <u>in</u>.
Don't muddle the two.

I learn.

Can you learn me to drive?

= WRONG

That's fine.

Can you <u>teach</u> me to drive?

Principal *and* Principle

This means '<u>first</u>' or '<u>main</u>'.

These are <u>morals</u> or <u>rules</u>.

The <u>principal</u> role was played by a man of <u>principles</u>.

Hmm — isn't skiving the opposite of learning...

<u>Borrowing</u> means <u>taking</u> something <u>from</u> someone else; <u>lending</u> means <u>giving</u> something <u>to</u> someone else. So 'John <u>lent</u> me his hat' is the same as 'I <u>borrowed</u> John's hat'. That's quite tricky, so <u>learn</u> it.

74

Revision Summary

This is a really nasty section. All of these mistakes are easy to make. You need to go through each page very carefully, to make sure that you don't miss out a single one. Getting these mistakes sorted now will make a big difference to your writing. Your work will be clear and you won't make any of those annoying little errors that give examiners a bad impression. Start by working through these smashing quick-fire questions, just to see exactly what you know, and what you need to spend more time learning. You know it makes sense.

1) What's the difference between 'practise' and 'practice'?
2) Write a sentences using 'practise'.
3) Write a sentence using 'practice'.
4) Write a sentence using 'advise'.
5) Write a sentence using 'advice'.
6) What's the difference between 'passed' and 'past'?
7) Write a sentence using 'passed' and another one using 'past'.
8) Write a sentence using 'affect' and another one using 'effect'.
9) What does 'accept' mean? What does 'except' mean?
10) Write a sentence using 'where', one using 'wear' and one using 'were'.
11) Write a sentence using 'there', one using 'their' and one using 'they're'.
12) What does 'to' mean?
13) What does 'two' mean?
14) What does 'too' mean?
15) Write one sentence using 'off' and another using 'of'.
16) What's wrong with this? 'The cat licked the milk off of the plate'.
17) Give the two correct ways of writing the sentence in question 16).
18) What's wrong with this? 'Give me them chips'. What should you put instead?
19) Write one sentence using 'them' properly. Remember — don't put it with a noun.
20) Write one sentence using 'those' properly.
21) What's the difference between 'lend' and 'borrow'?
22) Write a sentence using 'lend'. Write it again so that you can use 'borrow'.
    Think about who is doing the giving and who is doing the taking.
23) What's the difference between 'teach' and 'learn'?
24) Write a sentence using 'teach' properly.
25) What's the difference between 'principal' and 'principle'?
26) Write a sentence using 'principal'.
27) Write a sentence using 'principle'.
28) Write a short piece using any three of the pairs of confusing words from this section.
29) Write a short piece using three different sets of confusing words from this section.
30) Learn these ten words thoroughly, making totally sure you can spell them perfectly.

unconscious	occur	occurred	February	embarrass
restaurant	emotion	excitement	receive	immediately

An/And & Now/Know

This is a scary section. Not because it's hard, but because it's about the simplest, most obvious mistakes people make. That probably sounds a bit weird but you'll see exactly what I mean. These are the stupid mistakes you can make when you're in a hurry — and they're pretty bad ones.

Never Leave the '-d' Off 'And'

1) It's easily done and really stupid too — you end up writing 'an' instead of 'and'.

Hmmm, spicy.

Bob __an__ Ginger were drinking.

2) This looks horrible. It happens because you're in too much of a rush.

Bob __and__ Ginger were drinking.

3) That's better. It makes proper sense now.

Always check through your writing after you finish. Make sure all the 'and's have a '-d'.

It was milk __and__ mustard.

Don't Write 'Now' When You Mean 'Know'

Another gruesome mistake here — leaving the 'k' off 'know'.

He doesn't __now__ when to stop working.

This doesn't make any sense — 'now' means something else.

He doesn't __know__ when to stop working.

The only way to avoid mistakes is to think carefully before you write 'know'. Don't forget the 'k'.

'Know' has a 'k' you don't say, just like 'knee' and 'knickers'.

Lenin's lazy mistakes — always Russian things...

Lots of learning to do in this bit. Don't worry — there's nothing here that's very difficult. It's about silly mistakes like writing 'an' instead of 'and' or 'now' instead of 'know'. Definitely ones to avoid.

| 'Ask' & 'Feel' | # Ask/Aks and Fill/Feel |

These are <u>terrible</u> mistakes. They're the kind of thing that should make you <u>cringe</u>.
The <u>stupid thing</u> about them is they're caused by you <u>rushing</u>. All you need to do is <u>concentrate</u>.

You'll Kick Yourself If You Write 'Aks'

If you're writing in a hurry, this looks fine...

Make yourself useful, go and aks the way to the bank.

..but look more <u>closely</u> and it's complete <u>rubbish</u>. There's <u>no such word</u> as 'aks', even though some people use it when they <u>speak</u>.

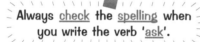

Make Sure You Write 'ASK' Properly

<u>Don't</u> muddle the letters, or miss out the 's'.

WRONG!

What if he <u>aks</u> me why I want to know?

What if he <u>asks</u> me why I want to know?

Always <u>check</u> the <u>spelling</u> when you write the verb '<u>ask</u>'.

When You Mean 'Feel', Don't Write 'Fill' Instead

Watch out — sometimes people put 'fill' when they <u>mean</u> 'feel'.
That's daft. It's only because they're <u>rushing</u>.

NO!

Deadlines made her <u>fill</u> annoyed.

This is a <u>dreadful</u> mistake. <u>Fill</u> means 'putting something in' — 'Fill it up.'

Deadlines made her <u>feel</u> annoyed.

Here's what you <u>meant</u> to write in the first place.

She asked how I feel — I said "With my fingers"...

These mistakes look <u>stupid</u> when they're written down like this. But when you're <u>rushing</u> to finish an essay in the middle of an exam, you can end up making them <u>without</u> thinking. That's a real <u>waste</u>. The examiners will think you're <u>sloppy</u> and that'll cost you <u>valuable marks</u>. <u>Learn</u> these rules instead.

Here/Hear and Been/Being

These words are much <u>harder</u>. It's a lot easier to <u>confuse</u> them, so look at this page <u>carefully</u>.

Use 'Have' With 'Been' But Never with 'Being'

1) You <u>can't</u> use 'been' on its own. You need '<u>have</u>', '<u>has</u>' or '<u>had</u>' with it.

I <u>been</u> to the pool. **= WRONG**

2) This is right — you've <u>got</u> to put the '<u>have</u>' in.   I <u>have been</u> to the pool.

3) You have to use '<u>being</u>' with '<u>is</u>', '<u>am</u>', '<u>are</u>', '<u>was</u>' or '<u>were</u>'.

He is <u>being</u> laughed at.

4) Sometimes you can have '<u>being</u>' on its <u>own</u> — but <u>never</u> 'been'.

Stop <u>being</u> scared.

Think Twice when You Write 'Here' or 'Hear'

HERE is like 'There'

Come <u>here</u>.

I'm not <u>here</u>.

<u>Here</u> they come.

HEAR — think 'Ear'

<u>Hear</u> the music.

Dogs can <u>hear</u> everything.

Can you <u>hear</u> it?

Don't <u>ever</u> mix up '<u>here</u>' and '<u>hear</u>'.
<u>Mistakes</u> like 'I can't here you,' or 'There's a snake in hear,' are plain <u>awful</u>.

Loud music — hear today, gone tomorrow...

'<u>Been</u>' and '<u>being</u>' follow a <u>simple rule</u>. You <u>can't</u> use 'been' unless there's a '<u>have</u>', '<u>has</u>' or '<u>had</u>' floating about with it. The <u>rest</u> of the time use '<u>being</u>'. For '<u>here</u>' and '<u>hear</u>', think '<u>there</u>' and '<u>ear</u>'.

| DON'T LEAVE OUT IMPORTANT 'O's | # Choice/Choose/Chose & Loose/Lose |

Sometimes <u>one tiny letter</u> can <u>change</u> the meaning of a word completely.
That's where <u>lots</u> of <u>mistakes</u> get made when you're trying to write in a <u>hurry</u>.

Don't Confuse 'Choose', 'Chose' and 'Choice'

This <u>looks</u> obvious enough — but it's a <u>common mistake</u>.
People write 'chose' <u>instead</u> of 'choose'.

You've got to <u>chose</u> the colour.

= WRONG

You've got to <u>choose</u> the colour.

<u>Don't</u> leave out an '<u>o</u>' because you're rushing.

Learn this now:

Choose = present tense

She <u>chooses</u> a new one every day.

Chose = past tense

She <u>chose</u> it last week.

Choice = noun

A metal toothbrush is a bad <u>choice</u>.

NO! <u>Never</u> put 'choice' in as a <u>verb</u>.

I can't <u>choice</u>, you decide for me.

I can't <u>choose</u>, you decide for me.

Watch Out for 'Loose' and 'Lose' too

It's dead easy to <u>miss out</u> an 'o'. Think <u>carefully</u> when you're using these words.

Loose = Not Tight

Lose = Opposite of Win
      Opposite of Find

Hurry up, or we'll <u>loose</u>!

= WRONG

Hurry up, or we'll <u>lose</u>!

This is right.

Trainspotting? — nah...choose life, pal....

'Choose' and 'chose', 'loose' and 'lose' are only ever confused because people <u>leave out</u> 'o's when they're in a <u>hurry</u>. If you stop and <u>think</u> about it, you'll <u>never</u> make these mistakes — so <u>think first</u>.

Our/Are and Him/Them

Here are <u>two hideous mistakes</u> to watch out for. <u>Don't</u> make these ones, whatever you do.

Never Write 'Our' as 'Are'

1) There's <u>no excuse</u> for this one. It's a really <u>stupid</u> mistake.

> This is <u>are</u> new pet.

2) 'Are' is a <u>verb</u> — you mean '<u>our</u>'.

> This is <u>our</u> new pet.

> <u>Our</u> is like <u>Your</u>
>
> <u>Are</u> is a <u>verb</u>

NO!

He's <u>ares</u>, not yours.

3) 'Ours' is <u>like</u> the word 'yours'.

He's <u>ours</u>, not yours.

Even Worse, Don't Put 'Him' When You Mean 'Them'

'<u>Them</u>' and '<u>him</u>' can <u>sound</u> similar when you're talking — 'Tell 'em to stop.' But they're <u>totally different</u> when you <u>write</u>. Don't ever <u>muddle</u> them up.

> He smiled at <u>him</u>.

Think about it — do you mean '<u>him</u>' or '<u>them</u>'?

> He smiled at <u>them</u>.

> They screamed at <u>them</u>.

Time to <u>think</u> again.

> They screamed at <u>him</u>.

THEM

HIM

> This little problem comes from writing <u>without</u> thinking.
> Get it <u>clear</u> — you can <u>avoid</u> this mistake easily.

Two rock and roll verbs — are and be...

You <u>must</u> make sure you <u>never</u> make either of these mistakes. '<u>Him</u>' and '<u>them</u>', '<u>are</u>' and '<u>our</u>' are so <u>different</u> that getting them wrong is very <u>embarrassing</u> as well as <u>stupid</u>. Just <u>learn</u> the page.

MORE SNEAKY SOUNDALIKES

Saw/Sore and Buy/By/Bye

It gets even <u>worse</u>, I'm afraid. Mistakes like these all <u>add up</u> to a bad impression and <u>bad marks</u>.

Don't <u>Write</u> 'Sore' when You Mean 'Saw'

1) This is a nasty, <u>lazy</u> mistake.

I <u>sore</u> him eating.

2) You've got to use '<u>saw</u>' — 'sore' <u>isn't</u> even a verb.

I <u>saw</u> him eating.

Use <u>SAW</u> for what you've <u>SEEN</u>.

<u>SORE</u> is about what <u>hurts</u>.

My head is <u>sore</u>.

'Buy', 'By' and 'Bye'

The secret here is to <u>learn</u> when to use '<u>buy</u>' and '<u>bye</u>'.
The rest of the time use '<u>by</u>'.

BUY as in shops

You can't <u>buy</u> love.

'<u>Buy</u>' with a 'u' means <u>getting</u> <u>something</u> in exchange for <u>money</u>.

You can't <u>by</u> love.

This is <u>wrong</u>.

BY is a joining word

'<u>By</u>' means '<u>on</u>', '<u>beside</u>' or '<u>by means of</u>'.

Let's go <u>by</u> bus.

= by means of...

NO!

Let's go <u>buy</u> bus.

Good-BYE

'<u>Bye</u>' is short for '<u>goodbye</u>'.

"<u>Bye</u>, lads!"

It's also an <u>extra run</u> in cricket — if the ball <u>passes</u> the batsman <u>without</u> being hit.

Four leg <u>byes</u> to England.

Buy me a dried-up river — they're dirt cheap...

<u>Learn</u> the different uses of '<u>buy</u>', '<u>bye</u>' and '<u>by</u>', and remember '<u>sore</u>' is a <u>pain</u>, '<u>saw</u>' is about <u>eyes</u>.

SECTION EIGHT — LAZY MISTAKES

Would/Wood and Close/Clothes

These ones are really <u>lazy mistakes</u>. They're the sort of thing that <u>ruins</u> your written work.

'WOULD' is like Could, but 'WOOD' is for Trees

I <u>wood</u> if I could.   = HORRIBLE

'Wood' <u>isn't</u> a verb. You need 'would' here.

I <u>would</u> if I could.

WOOD

'Would' <u>doesn't</u> mean a <u>place</u> or a <u>thing</u>. This time you really need '<u>wood</u>'.

He lived in the <u>wood</u>.

Never Write 'Close' Instead of 'Clothes'

This is <u>totally wrong</u>. You mean 'clothes'.

The Headmistress forgot to put her <u>close</u> on.

What's everyone laughing at?

<u>Don't</u> get these two words confused.

The Headmistress forgot to put her <u>clothes</u> on.

Clothes = what you wear
Close = to shut

His <u>close</u> were 'unusual'.

WRONG!

That's better. '<u>Clothes</u>' are the things he's <u>wearing</u>.

His <u>clothes</u> were 'unusual'.

The emperor's new clothes — they didn't suit him...

This stuff's incredibly <u>boring</u>, I know. Sadly, there's <u>no way</u> around it. These are such <u>ridiculous</u> mistakes — and they all come from <u>rushing</u> your work instead of making sure it's as <u>clear</u> as it can possibly be. <u>Learning</u> the mistakes to <u>avoid</u> is the <u>best way</u> to make sure you <u>never</u> make them.

82

A CROSS / ACROSS
A PART / APART

'Across' and 'Apart'

This is an annoying little mistake that really winds examiners up.
When you're in a rush, it's easy to write 'across' and 'apart' as if they're 'a cross' or 'a part'.

Don't Write 'Across' as 'A Cross' by Accident

This is wrong. It isn't what you want say. ➤ *I leapt a cross the ravine.*

I leapt across the ravine.

You've got to make it clear that 'across' is one word. Otherwise the sentence won't make sense.

'A cross' is just an 'X'.

'Across' means 'over' or 'on the other side of'.

She lives across the river.

The poison was marked with a cross.

It's the Same with 'Apart' and 'A Part'

This one doesn't make sense. *The Moon was empty a part from Ted.*

'Apart' is one word — don't let the 'a' drift away from the 'part', or the examiner'll think you mean something else.

The Moon was empty apart from Ted.

If you wrote this as two words, it'd sound like a car part or something.

They couldn't pull themselves apart.

Bad actors and actresses — can't get them a part...

It all seems so obvious, but that's why you've really got to cram this stuff into your mind. This is one of those mistakes that comes out of carelessness. Make sure you write words like 'across' clearly.

SECTION EIGHT — LAZY MISTAKES

Though/Through/Thorough

THREE TRICKY
'TH' WORDS

Uh oh — these words are really <u>nasty</u>. They <u>look</u> similar but they're all completely <u>different</u>.
If you're <u>rushing</u>, it's dead easy to slip in an <u>extra</u> 'o' by mistake. <u>Go over</u> this page very slowly.

Mind the <u>R's</u> in <u>Though</u>, <u>Thorough</u> <u>and</u> <u>Through</u>

though

He's light, even <u>though</u> he's big.

This is the <u>easiest</u> one to get right.
It's <u>like</u> 'although' — there's <u>no</u> 'r' in it.

through

They swam straight <u>through</u> me.

<u>Don't</u> miss out the '<u>r</u>' because you're <u>rushing</u>.

They swam straight <u>though</u> me. = **WRONG**

thorough

I got a <u>thorough</u> beating.

'Thorough' means '<u>complete</u>'. It has <u>two</u> 'o's.
<u>Don't</u> put 'through' by mistake.

Though, through, thorough — mind your 'r's...

Three words that you absolutely <u>must</u> learn. There's <u>no</u> other way to make sure you get them <u>right</u>.
'<u>Though</u>' is like '<u>although</u>'; '<u>through</u>' is a <u>direction word</u> and '<u>thorough</u>' means <u>complete</u>. Learn them.

84

No One/Nobody/Nothing/Nowhere

For some words, you've got to stick 'no' on the front to give the opposite, like 'nobody'.
The big secret is whether to write them as one word or two.

'No One' is Two Words, but 'Nobody' is One Word

1) These are the two everyone gets confused.

Noone was scared.

= WRONG

No one was scared.

2) You must write 'no one' as two words.
Don't write 'noone' or 'no-one'.

Look at his big red head!

3) 'Nobody' is always one word.

NO! ➤ No body was scared.

Nobody was scared.

'Everyone', 'Someone' and 'Anyone' are all One Word

someone   everyone   anyone

Anyone for turnip tennis?

These cheeky chaps are always single words if you're talking about people.
The only one that isn't is 'no one'.

Words Ending in '-thing', '-body', '-where' Follow a Pattern

Everything, everybody, everywhere.

They're all single words.

She went everywhere on her bike.

It's the same for 'Some', 'No' and 'Any' words.

There's nothing here.   somewhere   anybody

2, 3, 4, 5, 6, 7, 8, 9, 10 — no one there...

It's really very simple — 'no one' is two words, but 'nobody', 'nowhere' and 'nothing' are single words.

Two Words or One

Here are a few seriously <u>troublesome words</u>. They mean <u>one thing</u> if you write them as <u>one word</u>, and something <u>different</u> if you write them as <u>two words</u>. You need to <u>learn</u> to tell them <u>apart</u>.

Watch Out For These Tricky Words

1) 'Always' is a very common word — <u>don't confuse</u> it with 'all ways'.

He eats soup <u>always</u>.

= he does it every time.

He eats soup <u>all ways</u>.

= he does it in every different way.

'Always' means <u>every time</u>.
'All ways' means in <u>every different way</u>.

2) Another word you have to use a lot is '<u>altogether</u>'. Don't <u>muddle</u> it up with '<u>all together</u>'.

You're <u>altogether</u> wrong.

= completely.

She fixed three cars <u>altogether</u>.

= in total.

<u>Altogether</u> it was a success.

= on the whole.

BUT! ➡ **We were <u>all together</u> last year.**

= all of us were together.

3) These two are the <u>toughest</u> to get right.
<u>Never</u> write 'may be' when you mean 'maybe'.

I <u>may be</u> late.

= like 'I could/might be late'.

<u>Maybe</u> I won't.

= perhaps.

Watch your <u>handwriting</u> — make sure you leave <u>clear spaces</u> between words. That way your '<u>may be</u>' will be <u>clearly different</u> from your '<u>maybe</u>'. So do it.

These Words Are Only Written One Way — Learn Them

in fact
a lot **= two words**
thank you

today
tomorrow **= one word**

May be — nothing to do with mayflies...

<u>Learn</u> the <u>differences</u> between '<u>always</u>' & '<u>all ways</u>', '<u>maybe</u>' & '<u>may be</u>', '<u>altogether</u>' & '<u>all together</u>'.

Two More Tricky Pairs

Whether/Weather & Peace/Piece

Two more tricky pairs of words here. Make sure you get them clear before moving on.

'WEATHER' is Rain or Shine; 'WHETHER' Means If

Weather it's hot or cold. = WRONG

You really want to say 'if' here, so use 'whether'.

Whether it's hot or cold.

NO! *I love British whether.*

This time you're talking about the climate, so it must be 'weather'. *I love British weather.*

A 'Piece' is a Bit, but 'Peace' Goes with War

PIECE means 'part of'.

PEACE is the opposite of war.

WATCH OUT! *It's a peace of cake.*

It's a piece of cake.

That's better — 'piece' means bit.

What do you mean 'overcooked'?
FRUIT CAKE

Don't fall to pieces.

You mean 'little bits' here, so this is right.

OUCH! *I need piece and quiet.*

You need 'peace' here, not bits.

I need peace and quiet.

This is the opposite of war, so it's right.

'War and Peace' is a whopping great book.

John Lennon liked veg — he gave peas a chance...

'Piece' and 'peace' can definitely be a bit tricky to remember. Always think of this: 'piece' with an 'i' means bit. As for 'weather' and 'whether', learn the word 'weatherman' to get them straight.

A Big Spelling Hint

Phew — instead of more confusing words, this page is about one last big rule.
When you're writing an essay of any kind, don't change the way you spell a word as you go.

If You Aren't Sure, Try to Work Out the Spelling

This is another one of those problems that comes from rushing.
People start by spelling a word one way, and then change their mind later on.
Sometimes they start off spelling a word correctly, but get careless and spell it wrongly later.

> *The girl with the black belt beet me easily. She grabbed my collar and rolled me on to the matt. I jumped up, but she grabed my wrist and beat me against the matt again and againe.*

1) This looks terrible. It's been written by someone who can't make up their mind.

2) 'Mat' is spelt wrongly all the way through.

3) 'Beat', 'grabbed' and 'again' are spelt two different ways in the same paragraph.

4) If you spell words correctly as well as incorrectly, you'll lose marks for being careless.

5) The examiner can see that you know the right spellings, but you're too lazy to check through your work.

> Check your spellings through when you finish every piece of work.
> Don't leave different spellings of the same word.
>
> ## Choose one way and stick to it.

A reliable magician — that's consistent spelling...

Spelling is a funny business. It isn't the sort of thing that can ruin your marks completely, but it can really annoy the examiners — especially if it looks like you're just being lazy. It doesn't take long to check your spelling, and it's a great way to be sure your work makes a good impression.

Revision Summary

Just this final set of questions to work through. This is a strange section. It doesn't have any general rules like the others — it's about mistakes, nothing else. That makes it even more important that you get it straight in your mind now. Once you've learned this section, you should never make any of these mistakes again. That'll improve the standard of your writing straight away. Your course isn't just marked on spelling and grammar, but they affect the way examiners look at your work. If it's scruffy and full of mistakes, you aren't giving yourself much of a chance. Work your way through these questions — if you get stuck, go back over the pages again. But remember — you're doing this to improve your work. You're the one who'll get the benefit... as long as you put the effort in now.

1)   Write a sentence using the word 'and'.
2)   Write a sentence using the word 'an'.
3)   Write a sentence using the word 'know'.
4)   Write a sentence using the word 'now'.
5)   What's wrong with this sentence? *'I had no idea, so I decided to aks my brother.'*
6)   Give the correct form of the sentence in the last question.
7)   What's the correct form of 'ask' with 'he'?
8)   What's wrong with this sentence? *'Dean didn't fill very happy.'*
9)   Write a sentence using the word 'feel'.
10) Write a sentence using the word 'fill'.
11) What three words do you need to use with 'been'?
12) Write a sentence using 'been'.
13) Write a sentence using 'being'.
14) What's the difference between 'hear' and 'here'?
15) What's the difference between 'choose', 'chose' and 'choice'?
16) Give an example sentence for each word in question 15).
17) What's the difference between 'loose' and 'lose'?
18) Give an example sentence for 'loose' and also one for 'lose'.
19) Write a sentence using the word 'our'.
20) Write a sentence using the word 'are'.
21) What's the difference between 'sore' and 'saw'?
22) What's the difference between 'buy', 'by' and 'bye'?
23) What's the difference between: a) 'wood' and 'would'?   b) 'close' and 'clothes'?
24) What's the difference between: a) 'across' and 'a cross'?   b) 'apart' and 'a part'?
     c) 'though', 'through' and 'thorough'?
25) Which of these forms is right? Give the correct forms for the others:
     a) no body, b) noone, c) everyone, d) some where, e) anyone, f) every body.
26) Write a sentence using each of these words: a) 'maybe', b) 'altogether', c) 'always'.
27) Write a sentence using each of these phrases: a) 'may be', b) 'all together', c) 'all ways'.
28) What's the difference between: a) 'weather' and 'whether'?   b) 'piece' and 'peace'?
29) What's the most important thing to remember about the way you spell words in your work?
30) Learn these ten useful words off by heart, and especially how to spell them.

| absence | temporary | successful | occasionally | independent |
| irrelevant | build | forty | permission | solemn |

Index

90

Index

Don't forget our other great value Revision Guides —

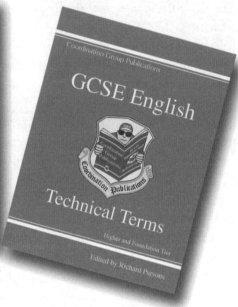

GCSE English — Writing Skills
96 Pages, Full Colour,
EFE4 — £3.50 (£2.00 for Schools)

KS3 English — Essential Terms
48 Pages, Full Colour,
EET3 — £3.00 (£1.50 for Schools)

GCSE English — Technical Terms
48 Pages, Full Colour,
ETT4 — £3.00 (£1.50 for Schools)

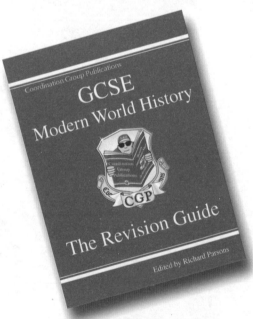

GCSE Modern World History —
The Revision Guide,
112 Pages, Full Colour,
HWR4 — £3.50 (£2.00 for Schools)

GCSE Schools History Project —
The American West & Medicine Through Time
84 Pages, Full Colour,
HPM4 — £3.50 (£2.00 for Schools)